THE SOUTHERN POETRY ANTHOLOGY

VOLUME IV

LOUISIANA

FIRST EDITION, 2011

Requests for permission to reproduce material from this work should be sent to:

> Permissions
> Texas Review Press
> English Department
> Sam Houston State University
> Huntsville, TX 77341-2146

Cover design and photo by Chad M. Pelton

A brief word about the below information: The Library of Congress directed us to use the CIP data from the first volume of the anthology, even though we have distinct data for volumes two and three. The correct publication information is listed below, before this data:

Title: *The Southern Poetry Anthology, IV: Louisiana*
Editors: William Wright and Paul Ruffin
ISBN-13: 978-1-933896-77-9
ISBN-10: 1-933896-77-9

Library of Congress Cataloging-in-Publication Data

The Southern poetry anthology : South Carolina / [compiled] by Stephen Gardner and
William Wright ~ 1st ed.
    p. cm.
  ISBN-13: 978-1-933896-06-9 (pbk. : alk. paper)
  ISBN-10: 1-933896-06-X (pbk : alk. paper)
  1. American poetry~South Carolina. I. Gardner, Stephen. II. Wright, William, 1979-
  PS558.S6S68 2007
  811.008'09757~dc22
                        2007023711

THE SOUTHERN POETRY ANTHOLOGY

VOLUME IV

LOUISIANA

William Wright, *Series Editor*

Paul Ruffin & William Wright, *Volume Editors*

PREVIOUS VOLUMES
OF THE SOUTHERN POETRY ANTHOLOGY

William Wright, Series Editor

Volume I: South Carolina
Edited by Stephen Gardner and William Wright

ISBN-10: 193389606X
ISBN-13: 978-1933896069

Volume II: Mississippi
Edited by Stephen Gardner and William Wright

ISBN-10: 1933896248
ISBN-13: 978-1933896243

Volume III: Contemporary Appalachia
Edited by Jesse Graves, Paul Ruffin, and William Wright

ISBN-10: 1933896647
ISBN-13: 978-1933896649

FORTHCOMING

Volume V: Georgia (Projected for 2012)
Edited by Paul Ruffin and William Wright

Volume VI: Tennessee (Projected for 2013)
Edited by Jesse Graves, Paul Ruffin, and William Wright

The editors dedicate this volume
to the memory of Maxine Cassin

1927-2010

FOREWORD

Louisiana's poets are remarkably generous. As I worked to design this collection, more and more I found that many writers here champion a sense of togetherness, a close-knit literary kin who share—whether at present or in memory—a profoundly beautiful and unique area of the United States. This communal aspect of Louisiana poets is typified by Maxine Cassin's literary legacy, both in her poems and in others' works she encouraged and fostered, in Darrell Bourque's selfless support of the state's writers, evidenced in his introduction that follows, and in John Freeman, who continues to find and support fresh voices.

This sense of community is most evident in the poetry, and in savoring this collection several times, I noticed recurrent patterns and tendencies: First, many Louisiana poets are relatively comfortable with form, and, by extension, formalism. The reasons for this are manifold, but one factor is especially notable: Form gives order. In Louisiana, more than any other area of the American South, order is precious, particularly in a time when disorder, natural or man-made, has destroyed much of the beauty Louisiana poets hold dear. Poetry serves as one ideal form to make sense of this disarray, a verbal counter to chaos and a simultaneous homage to poetry of the past and the oral tradition that informs it. In this way, form is created and preserved, even if many qualities of the past on which it depends have been lost.

I also found Louisiana poetry preoccupied, like much of the South, with nature and natural motifs. Distinguishing Louisiana's poetry, however, is a prevalent thematic fixation on water. Water—whether storms, hurricanes, rain showers, ponds, lakes, creeks, or seascapes—is the central image with which many Louisiana poets meditate on the changeability and unpredictability of the environment, the hope for renewal, and the mutability of identity.

Finally, the motif of water leads me to fecundity—a word that resonates strongly in these poems. Louisiana poetry delights in the fertility of the land, the give and take of soil and sea, the warm womb that spawns a landscape rife with lush complexity. Undoubtedly, this beautiful landscape informs Louisiana poets' successes in balancing sound and sense, sonically sophisticated poems motivated by explorations of self and the importance of place. This celebration of fecundity anticipates dynamic resurgences of ravaged places, the inevitability of new life sprung from decay.

This volume would not exist in its present form without the generosity of Louisiana's poets. I consider this literary community a source of inspiration—not merely through the beautiful works included herein, but in the manner its members love and help each other while inhabiting this underappreciated, often misunderstood literary genre. Paul Ruffin and I appreciate this particular community's support to create this book, a convivial *fête* we are confident will resound throughout Louisiana, the South, and beyond.

William Wright
Marietta, GA

INTRODUCTION

"And its look, rude, unbending, lusty, made me think of myself."
—Walt Whitman, "I Saw in Louisiana a Live-Oak Growing"

Contemporary Louisiana poetry is as rooted in rich literary history as it is in geography. Our poets are the kin of gigantic imaginations, as wild and unruly as they are tenacious. Our collective voice or timbre is shaped by the rich, sensitive, diverse, fecund, and troublesome geography in which we locate ourselves.

Louisiana poets work in an environment of rare literary energy. We write next to contemporary giants in other genres like Shirley Ann Grau, Ernest J. Gaines, Tony Kushner, William Joyce, and Richard Ford. Louisiana literary history is fueled by the energies of writers who came to Louisiana to sharpen their sensibilities and launch their careers: Lafcadio Hearn, Kate Chopin, Sherwood Anderson, William Faulkner, F. Scott Fitzgerald, Tennessee Williams, and Walker Percy.

And then there are the past's poets among us: Pinkie Gordon Lane, the first African-American to receive a Ph.D. from Louisiana State University and the first African-American Louisiana Poet Laureate (1989-1992). We rightfully stake claim to an association with the work and legacy of Robert Penn Warren, twice the United States Poet Laureate, who won two Pulitzer Prizes in poetry and one in fiction, who wrote the influential texts, *Understanding Poetry* and *Understanding Fiction*, and who co-founded and edited (1935-1942) *The Southern Review* with Cleanth Brooks when he was on the Louisiana State University faculty (1934-1942). Part of our poetic identity is linked to Bob Kaufman (1925-1986), born in New Orleans to a black Catholic mother from Martinique and a German Orthodox Jew. In the 1940s Kaufman traveled to New York City where he met Allen Ginsberg and William Burroughs, and then to San Francisco, where he joined Gregory Corso, Jack Kerouac, and Lawrence Ferlinghetti and became part of the influential Beat scene. Kaufman founded *Beatitude* magazine in 1955. In Europe, and especially in France, Kaufman was known as "the American Rimbaud." And, not least, there is Walt Whitman, who tried his hand at being a journalist in New Orleans for a few months in 1945. And while the journalism job did not work out, his description of the oak in his famous Louisiana poem could be a description of Louisiana poetry itself: "live-oak glistens there in Louisiana, solitary, in a wide flat space. . . ."

One of the most active and generous advocates for contemporary Louisiana poetry was Maxine Cassin (1927-2010), to whom this volume of *The Southern Poetry Anthology* is dedicated. A philosophy graduate of Newcomb College, she began as a formal, philosophical poet who went on to publish four books of poems: *A Touch of Recognition*, 1962; *Turnip's Blood*, 1985; *The Other Side of Sleep*, 1995; and *Against the Clock, New and Neglected Poets*, 2003. Besides writing poems, Cassin dedicated much of her time to the poetry of others, at first through her work with Richard Ashman in the 1950s on the *New Orleans Poetry Journal*, whose distinguished contributors included James Wright, William Stafford, Sylvia Plath, Donald Hall, and Vassar Miller. After the journal ceased publication, she published individual volumes over five decades as publisher and editor of the *New Orleans Poetry Journal* Press (including works by Miller, Everette Maddox, founder of the legendary Maple Leaf Bar poetry reading series, Ralph Adamo, and Charles deGravelles). She also published Malaika Favorite's poetry and art, Clarence John Laughlin's photographs, and, with Maddox and Yorke Corbin, edited the first *Maple Leaf Rag* anthology. The last book of poetry she published, Dale Matthews' *Wait for the Green Fire*, appeared only a few months before her death. And we have not yet heard the last of Cassin's voice: there is much of hers we've yet to discover.

Her dedication and resolve to promote poetry is beautifully captured in her poem "Determination" (in the volume *Turnip's Blood*) in which she so closely resembles the chameleon of the poem, chased and lost "among the roses," while retaining the voice of the speaker:

> The thorn in my flesh
> asks to remain embedded—
> now so much a part of me
> I shall not be undefended
> from whatever finds its way
> beneath my skin.

In addition to the rich intellectual and philosophical threads woven throughout the sensibilities of Louisiana's contemporary poets are the interminable and undeniable essences of the earth. We are a people and a culture of the land. Even our urban areas define themselves in accordance to landscape: Our great city of the coast sits precariously below sea level, a fact that contributes greatly to its identity. Our great river, whose Ojibwa name *Mississippi* means just that, defines much of who and what we are. Our vanishing coastline is an urgent catalyst to poems and visual art. Our lesser rivers, the Atchafalaya, the Red River, and the Sabine shape our wetland designations and nature-consciousness from the northern borders to the Gulf of Mexico. Our lesser waters, like the bayous Lafourche and Teche, serve as ancient conduits that continue to characterize the culture of Louisiana Cajuns. The Kisatchie National Forest and the "hill" country above it sharpen our connection to the Native Americans who forever reside in cultural memory. In the truest sense, our poetry is indicative of a Creole nation: We are a mix of Native American clans and tribes, the ancestors of slaves, the descendants of free persons of color; we are Vietnamese-Americans and Haitian-Americans, German-Americans, British-Americans, French-Americans. We are prairie people and bayou people, forest people and hill people, as well as citizens of great cities. We are poets of the countryside and of urbanity, poets of the street and poets who dwell in the state's academies. We are poets who have stayed put, poets who have but barely left the confines of our borders, and poets who have come from outside to live and work within. We may hold a national distinction in that citizens of Acadiana often refer to people living outside the region as *les Américains* even as they hold fierce loyalty to the ideals of the mother country. We may be home to one of the rarest cities in the world, New Orleans, with its great centers of learning, with its gumbo cultures, with its mysterious ability to let genuine refinement and decadence co-exist. Our poetry is made of this mix, this *mélange* that always sounds like jazz, like song, like poem.

Among the ninety-seven poets represented in this anthology are natives who still live and work in the state. Jack B. Bedell is a great poetry proponent as the editor of *Louisiana Literature* and co-editor of *French Connections: A Gathering of Franco-American Poets*. Heather Ross Miller, in her commentary about his *Come Rain, Come Shine*, praises his poems as "[H]igh-spirited and unafraid, full of Louisiana Cajun zest, quick to anger and quick to forgive, and quick to offer unabashed praise for this world. . . ." John Biguenet repeatedly balances intellectual acuity with sensuous detail and David Middleton explores the spiritual through tangible reality. And each of these master poets offer the reader every kind of formal variation imaginable, the formalities never merely peripheral but integral to the poem and testament to their genius. Gina Ferrara is such a poet; as is Mona Lisa Saloy; Keagan Lejeune from Lake Charles; John Doucet from Thibodaux and Lafourche Parish; and Barry Ancelet, Caroline Ancelet, and Zachary Richard from Acadiana.

Many of Louisiana's poets have had to leave the region. Among them, the saucy, witty, wonderful David Kirby, who ties intelligence to levity and sincerity to unguarded affection. There are few poets in the world whose wide net, often filled with barbs, embraces so completely and pleasurably. Kevin Meaux's poems long for the passing beauties of the world and for the ways this beauty offers itself to us repeatedly. Sheryl St. Germain writes of addiction, abuse, desire, and falling headlong into the life she has been given. Her poems document her love of the earth, a poetic crossroads where art meets the call for responsible citizenry head-on. An equally great earth-writer is Martha Serpas, whose poems quest for spiritual entry. Hers is the work of a metaphysician. Serpas' poetic tropes are more than glued to our notions of how and what those things are in the world; they are also meditations and probes into the human mind, the human heart, human action and its consequences.

Among the most magical, searing, and probing voices in Louisiana poetry is the voice of Yusef Komunyakaa. Born in Bogalusa, Louisiana, Komunyakaa became one of America's greatest war poets with the publication of *Dien Cai Dau* (1988), an expression and articulation which continue through his recent *Warhorses* (2008). His *Neon Vernacular: New and Selected Poems* was the winner of the 1994 Pulitzer Prize. In 2007, Lt. Governor Mitch Landrieu presented Komunyakaa with the Louisiana Writer Award.

The state's body of poetry is enriched by the many poets who have come to us from other regions. Julie Kane, a winner of the Donald Justice Prize, has lived and worked in Louisiana for over three decades; her formal poetry is adventurous, brave, and unrelentingly frank in its investigations of the human condition. Catharine Savage Brosman's keen intelligence and lively heart gird themselves on equally lively and disarming formalism. Ava Leavell Haymon's sustained production is testament to her commitment to art, her commitment to continuing a dialog about the complexities of communication through and beyond myth, fairytale, and storytelling. John Gery's poems are perfectly at ease in formal expression without conspicuous formal scaffolding. Biljana D. Obradovic, a Serbian-American poet, offers penetrating, powerful, and disarming glimpses into American culture. Experimental poet Marthe Reed essentializes the idiosyncratic in her work. Adding their distinctive voices to Louisiana poetry are John Freeman, Denise Rogers, Peter Cooley, David Havird, and Ashley Mace Havird; each one of them teacher-poets whose bodies of poetry vary from single volumes to multiple volumes and whose work as poets and teachers make for the strong writing programs we have in the state.

The poets mentioned in this introduction are but a representation of what Louisiana poetry offers. Among the unnamed contributors to this volume are fine ekphrastic poets and bold experimentalists. Some are elegists, some clarionists, some documentarians of both natural and man-made disaster and disorder of recent times. And all, the named and the unnamed, are explorers of the big themes that literature calls us to: identity, culture, and the great experiment of living in the world, living with ourselves, and living with each other.

Darrell Bourque
St. Landry Parish, Louisiana

11

CONTENTS

16

RALPH ADAMO

New Orleans Elegies

I

The shape of the loss is fretted but not mapped.
You cannot say 'Elenore' and have it so, nor 'Lindell.'
But pluck the unpromising chord, pull back
the hammer, pour the residual face, listen:
an ancient bridge emerges from your heart
across whose stone logs a loud commerce rattles
day and night, of earnings lost in sport,
lives waged against a broken treadle,
the sunny loneliness of the next drink,
a picturesque adhesion at the core
where all the voices versed against the blank
look crap out, and once more you've gone to war.

II

All work is not the same as the work of love
when the mind changes, as it does now,
looking up in a room suddenly not quiet—
the trill of comprehension from her page
a sound like madness—reasonable, familiar—
close enough to mine but still not touching.
But love is shy work, the clapper in a bell.
I should be scared to talk, with what I've said.

Does love press an image in her page,
this desiccated, wakeful old celebrant
of the invisible, breaking the law
with her mind that levels language,
with her eyes that cannot light anywhere,
with her hands that rip god out of your throat—
why would her meekness not terrify me?

III

Once or twice in the song I swear I was sleeping,
my head hanging from a single thread that no longer

looked much like luck or the formula for dreams,
the shy end of her toward me, a festival, a borrowing.

Once in the clear of the melody one loses the key,
it is impossible to lock the music up, a theme strikes
that this one is still helpless to close or open
although there seems to be no trick to it, no joke.

Always it yields in time to be forgotten.
I wish once we could sleep like two horses
standing side by side after a twilight feed,
eyes lashed for the night, forelegs atremble,

but just barely, with being so strongly still.

Gift of the Guest

Winter of sorrow, you arrive
and take your place at the window.
At first we do not speak.
You stand there looking out, you borrow my clothes freely.
I'm busy with my contract
to smash and cart away statuary
cast during the previous administration.
Time is short and wasting.
There's tons of the other stuff,
its gaudy paint barely dry.
You don't notice how hard I work,
or I wouldn't have to cook supper for both of us.
It's true you never eat, never leave the window
(when I'm around) and do not lift your hands
except to make odd gestures
that ignore the text of my conversation.
It's true you leave me alone.
I don't know why you have come.
The birds do not interest you,
and you don't hear the children when they call up to you
walking home from school.
The trees seem to grow more bare and introspective
at your glance, itself unintentional,
like the many times you shatter the window with your tongue.
You only look at me one time,

and that time my face is thick with plaster.
You speak then, slowly, letting my blue robe fall
from your shoulders.
"You have made me laugh very much," you say.
"In return I will leave you this table."
And you go, and by the window is the table I have always had.

Us, Here, Ruled

I don't know if this sort of thing
can happen in other states
but today, on a raised platform
at Ground Zero of Lakeside
Shopping Center, it's Queen's Day
when the queens of many things and places
within the state of Louisiana
have gathered to tell the stopped shoppers—
the 'ladies and gentlemen' of their
practiced speech—where they are from
and what each of their names is
in a loud voice with a similar ring,
before grouping together under a sea
of crowns to sing "when the saints
go marching in," an anthem
sort of, for those of us who've
never been anywhere, who just
won't go, who'd rather be subjects
of the Shrimp & Petroleum Festival
Queen, or—really—the tall dark-
haired woman tightly poured in red
whose label, which she alone seems
shy of wearing, proclaims her
Queen of New Orleans, that one,
whom I have not yet begun
to learn how to address. . .
or the barefoot Queen of Pines
who's just now noticing it's half price
day at Nine West, busily seeks
respite from regality
in the common quest.

EMILY ALLEN

Apology

The evergreens cringe white over open wounds—
a disused rail line slit down into bedrock, raw
earth smothered with snow. I remember

when someone dumped a body near the old trestle,
hidden in a drift: Red and blue lights
caught on every edge, fragmenting with the frost.

We watched the scene fade slowly into darkness,
turned to the other and said what we meant.
You left without leaving a note, sometime

before first light. I wanted to be buried
with the quiet of flakes, disguised
and protected. I was afraid the thaw would leave

no trace of you, only the earth, visible and needy,
but now the sun's glint spotlights
every scar carved like a limestone vein.

Blame winter and the way it smells
of gunmetal against the teeth. Blame
stillness, the deadweight of ice.

Field Trip

We took the school bus as far as the road would let us, the wheels'
motion throwing us into each others' sharp elbows, or metal
so hot we jerked from the burn. We were three to a seat,

and potholes marked where floodwaters had almost washed
the route away, but as long as we were still moving,
we loved the jolting, like an amusement park ride.

When the teachers told us the road stopped here,
that we would have to walk into the hanging forest
of moss and rot, I still felt rolling movement. I wanted to run.

Under the cover of cypress, the heat was boiling. My sweat
was thick as the air, and every breath felt like drowning.
It was a large-scale effort, this swamp sweep:

We continued two by two into the darkness,
armed with pointed sticks to pick up trash along the water's
edge. Someone kept casting a net too large for fish.

We were supposed to clean, make this place pretty
for little reward, and I kept thinking it was a lost cause—everything
would return in the end to Styrofoam cups and faded beer cans.

Suddenly the net-caster shouted for someone to look
at what he'd found: an old Frigidaire, rusted the red-brown
color of swampwater, and shut tight with a padlock.

It dragged the bottom as they hauled it in, and the mud plowed
from the depths smelled worse than death. The afternoon
swarmed with flies trying to burrow between the freezer's hinges,

and the forest darkened like a screened-in porch at dusk.
The cloud pulsed and fractured, danced around us.
Our silence magnified their buzzing,

and I knew what no one was saying. They told us it was time to leave.
We walked with the swamp's stink heavy in our nostrils,
each step weighted with the give of the earth, mud's slow release.

The Necessity of Movement

I felt at home abroad—something about the isolation
of mountains, like a lighted window on the open plain.
When I returned, I missed trains: sleeping
through entire countries, waking up to the grind of brakes
and shuffling seatmates, being ringed in by the Pyrenees.

I condemned wasted space, the way that even after
seven hours over the Atlantic, when the turbulence
jolted me awake, I was thirty thousand feet above
rural Maine, and still two thousand miles from home.
As we dropped beneath the cloud cover, I saw

the edges curl and fold away and the ground
came to meet me like a lover determined to leave.
It is so seductive, the roll of the prairie; I've heard
Americans conceive of identity as open space,
like an intimate knowledge of earth's curvature.

One could drive forever and see no home more fixed
than a trailer sewn to the land with spiders' thread,
find no confidence in fences and piled bricks. This is my lot,
roughly a quarter acre square: A small house
and an overgrown garden facing the city's electric haze.

All I can see are rooflines, high windows, but I've learned
to navigate this sea of lights, identifying each pinprick
in the darkness by name, like a ship's captain steering
by the stars. He knows the push of waves and wind,
the threat in the shallows, and the inevitable turn of the tide.

LOU AMYX

Henna

Even a black t-shirt is warm,
tabled by the sidewalk, in front of the shops
where sunrays worm among the snaking limbs
of the one great tree. You hold my fingers
to turn my arm
as your other hand obscures it
in dark skin-staining squeezings,
patiently uncurling designings
inspired, you explain, by my earrings,
my earlobe, the place where
the thin winter light
enters my eye.

Two days before Christmas
and time is
these rows of dragonscales,
this circle of hearts,
the slow, handpainted length of an arm
and one palm, two fingers,
my entire right thumb.

You stand to shake the cloth out
as a weatherly breeze rushes in
and the day becomes,
not this tattoo, but
your laugh behind the flying cloth,
the skin near your flying skirt hem,
tiny bells somewhere, bracelets,
this mild southern winter when we met,
where even a black t-shirt is warm.

City Barbershop Burns

My father stood steady as he could
On the sidewalk across the street
Looking into the fire.
He could not focus on the men
Fighting the flames, though he felt
Their shadows crossing the glow.
He did not look left to see
The tears in the eyes
Of his wife of fifty years.
His gaze was locked on the inferno,
Struggling quietly, desperately
To make out the shape of the chair
Around which he had worked
And walked and listened and talked,
To build a home,
To feed a family,
To make a life.
The smoke in his eyes blurred the lines,
But his memory restored them
Just long enough to nod
Toward the ghastly glow.
He could not have imagined
That his farewell would be whispered
Under his breath from across the street
In the middle of the night.

CAROLINE ANCELET

My Brother in the Water

After your cremation,
the children and wife you had forsaken
divided your ashes—
gray dust and sharp bone shards
and put them God knows where.

I wish I had been given a handful
to sprinkle in the brown water
of Grand Isle
where the image of you
seining in the broken yellow sun-glints
emerges in negative light—
what I see after the bulb flashes
before you fade away.

You are all-enduring as you drag
the windblown net against
the weight of the water
rushing through the holes,
that far-off look in your gray eyes
already gazing toward oblivion
while Grandma and the rest of us
play Indian poker—
sticking cards to our damp foreheads
and placing bets on what we can't see.

Picture This

My grandfather arrived on a two-prop plane
from New Orleans, where he'd left the young mistress
we wouldn't find out about until after his death.
He fished peppermints out of his pockets for me,
and I knew what my father would look like as an old man.
He rarely spoke on the long road
to my grandmother's house.
When his lower legs clotted
to the color of dried port
she banished him to the tiny attic
room where his life sloped
like the walls into the musty eaves.
She tucked him away like some naked secret
sewn to her bosom.
At night, he sprinkled his sheets with water
to relieve the heat.
Her heart's bloody shutters
slammed closed to the smell of mentholatum.
She didn't want to see him
peel the bandages from his purple onion legs.
The odor of his parakeets,
his only companions, disgusted her.
They perched loyally on his bald head
as he carefully razored articles
from the newspapers, and tucked them
into the worn leather pouch
he'd carried through two world wars.
He came and went for years.
When his mistress called to say he'd had a stroke,
my father went to bring him home.
He climbed the circular stairs to the attic
to sort his father's belongings.
He opened the heavy leather pouch and found
among political cartoons, newspaper stories of war and of oil,
and wedding pictures of total strangers,
a picture of himself as a sepia child astride a new bicycle,
and one of him hugging Esso, their terrier,
and one of the women he'd just met in New Orleans,
smiling here, and young.
Seeing the picture my father remembered
having met her years before
as a receptionist in his father's

Canal Street office,
having flirted with her,
having, in fact, asked her out.
He couldn't understand then why she had refused him.
Now here she was, tucked away
with the clippings, these photos,
and, carefully wrapped in handkerchiefs,
every bird who'd ever sat atop his gentle father's head.

JOHN ANDERSON

Three Things

There are three things you can never get back,
my father always told me. The spent arrow,
the spoken word, and the missed opportunity.

He drew the song out with his fingertips
releasing words into the air for me to catch
—or try to. History too faint for me to hear.

Like his father before, he pantomimed
the words, honoring those gestures, important
as wilderness and path, father and son.

I still see the string of his bow drawn tight
against his eyes. Squinting, concentrating
beyond the sun, a mark I could never follow.

Setting aside the bow, he held up his open palms,
shrugged, waiting for the sound of a lesson
learned. I waited, too. I didn't understand

how hands so heavy could rein leather
tight as lightning yet fall soft and loose as rain.
Funny how all three things keep coming back.

Girl with Hairy Armpits Asked Me to the Prom

She was a pure, natural ugly,
though Pop would say there's no such thing.
Just some girls is prettier than others.
Every other girl in every other county—
hell, country—was more pretty, I thought.

She could play a brick between her knees
standing or walking. Her Virginia Slim accent
wasn't as advertised: It ran like honey,
weeks dried to the edge of the kitchen counter.
And what it touched stayed touched.

She knocked on my front door the day of the dance.
No one would've blamed me—not Pop, even she said so—
if I said no. I wanted to say yes, hairy armpits and all.
And to hell with that TL Adelai—
he wasn't going hunting anymore than I
was going to push that word up past dumb lips.
I shrugged, stuffed my hands down my pockets,
leaned against that doorframe,
cool against my burnt up blood, said, "Nah," and heard
Pop's chair inside push back heavy from the kitchen table.

I waited for the sound of her leaving, watching her
big feet not move, wishing I had on my own boots.
She leaned towards me then, way forward and low
and glitter filled my eyes—I could almost taste her
peroxide hair, feel her two lips breathe. Almost
peed my pants. That she whispered
too low for me to hear, didn't matter. I saw
everything. Everything she was about.
Everything I wanted: defined
under that thank-God, low-cut, white t-shirt.

I felt red whip-crack and spread across my sight
until I was no longer able to see any other color.
Even now, I still feel the red side of her hand, still hear
Pop excusing himself, having to fix something,
some place—any place—else.

The Blueberry Song

Blueberries bellow out round, ripe notes,
ringing loud and cool and blue,
clinging to white stars, conjuring
inky fingers swollen by blue lips
and ravenous blue days where
blackbirds beat their black wings blue.

This is the day the blueberries ring out
the blueberry women: wide and round
and ripe as blue bubbles,
balancing their blueberry baskets
upon their blueberry hips, swinging
loud and cool and round, rolling
blue songs from off the tips of blue tongues
underneath the blueberry branches
and rattling black feathered wind.

And this is the day the blueberry women
bring out the blueberry girls,
tied tight to blue apron string hips,
with blueberry knees and ripening blue lips,
all rabbit-eyed and wringing out blue notes
from blue flesh into blue juice, breaking
the round and wine of blue mouths
mouthing blue kisses, impressing blue tongues,
learning to sing the blueberry song.

And this is the day the blueberry girls sing out
the blueberry boys, and, oh, I'd be
a blueberry boy running and fetching
and wringing again the midnight fruit,
to pluck and cup blue morning dew,
and roll their blue sweetness between
my blue thumbs, blue fingers, blue tongue,
as the blackbirds cry Blue
and the berries cry Blue
and the branches cry Oh lord, blue
breaking underneath the blue weight
of blue tears tearing into blue skin
as the blueberry girls blossom
into blueberry women, and I,
into a blueberry man.

RANDY BATES

Dolphin Island

*—Now locally pronounced Dauphin (Daw' fn) Island, Ile Dauphine is in the Gulf
of Mexico near the Alabama coast. In 1699 the French-Canadian explorer
Pierre Le Moyne d'Iberville named the island for the many human skeletons he
found on its beaches. In 1708 Jean-Baptiste Le Moyne de Bienville changed the
name in an effort to console the dauphine who, in France, was mourning the
death of her mother.*

The first to mark this shore with French leather:
His gold compass eye finds bones banked in sand.
He spits, returns to the skiff. *Ile du Massacre.*

D'Iberville two years dead, his younger brother
renames the island. *Un geste politique.*
The dauphine continues to grieve for her mother.

*

The summer that x-rays found shadows
swimming in my mother's lung, I stayed here,
at her father's house, in a place I mistook
to be named after dolphins, a haven from sharks.
No bones lay in the sand, just trash
and bleached ship boards, things I still see
strewn beyond the three of us as we wandered out
where the salt heat was hard to look through.

*

Grandpa's a small man. He waves his cigar.
James, the black giant who stinks of storage and port,
is clowning before him. Grandpa shows fists,
then starts to shout *right!* and throws dollars
for each of the heavyweight champs that we name.
One of his biceps can dance like an egg.

James' wine-yellowed eyes seem to reckon my winnings
and how he might steal them. Nights he dreams sharks
at his cot, acts twice shrewd when I pay him
to give me his chore dragging in crab traps.

35

He'll never know the charm isn't his:
I've seen dolphins passing these breakers.

Other days crest into afternoon.
Three minds awash and nothing to say.
Grandpa's the lord in scenes James rehearses.
I think about wrecks, beasts, and beasts' play.

                    *

Today we dragged the traps in at sunset
near dolphins rolling down the shoreline.
Our son cried *sharks!* He wouldn't believe
what I told him. Not even at our bonfire
until I drank wine and mixed facts with myths
about dolphins and whale talk. His eyes leaped
at the waves when I described the shark's brain
but the word *bottle-nose* made him smile again.

The island's other names remained buried.
Acquisition, slaughter, the bereft dauphine,
they're tales for different seasons; for tonight
we've had pleasure, years make it clear:
crabs' claws, the weather band, stars.
Radio Mystery Theatre in darkness,
then baseball from Texas and cards
with cracked faces in sepia light.

                    *

My shadow on the screens of our rented cottage
now reflects the depth of this moonless night
before I give it back in watery toasts
in the names of slaves and dead kin.
Nothing left but to re-cover the children,
then come to sleep at their mother's breast.
I clasp her bones as the Gulf crashes.
Creatures, leaving voices, circle our beds.

Meteors

1

Before another death
let's drive again
slowly along the blacktop
through hay fields
and bars of gold light.
We need motion
to lighten our silence,
to help us believe
our old car belongs
among the shadows it catches
as we cross and re-cross the river,
the road rising into dusk
toward a one-street town
where the mountains begin.

2

High mirrors reflect
beer signs, billiards
the screen clapping to.
Cowhands in bowling shirts
laugh down lonesome music.
TV news melts in blue ice
on the bartop's ruined grain.
Tonight families arrive.
Someone begins to sing
the small things of this world,
as if we are safe.
When we leave The Chrome Bar
someone will wave.

3

As in another autumn
we lie by slowed water
to watch the Perseids
streak panes of sky
from Pegasus to Cetus.
Their flares are like mica

or a snail's track
before they are gone.
We shudder, wondering how
we dare leave children
the truths of distance,
our prayers to plain stone.

4

This is Grandpa's river
our son told us in spring.
They stood here, skipping rocks
that spattered the water,
then chipped sparks at midstream
from a ridged glacial bar.
Before another death
come through the clearing
to our frayed canvas room.
Let its doors fall open
and nothing fall between us
and our old burning parents,
the stars.

JACK B. BEDELL

Elvin Jones at Midnight

There are nights when I have complete control
of the stereo, nights when I can put on Coltrane
without my wife's face dropping into a frown.

Those nights, I can step to the backdoor
with the inexcusable pleasure of Elvin Jones
harassing the snare with his left hand,

tickling more sound out of his cymbals
than any one limb should be able to get,
and kicking just enough ahead of the beat

to make the whole band chase his time.
There's an undertone of harmony
in Jones' kit I know I'll have to explain

to my sons one day, hopefully in moonlight,
hopefully soon. I'll load them into the golfcart
with drinks and clubs and a jambox, take them

out onto the ninth green behind our house
and let them loose to do whatever damage they can
out of earshot of their mother. I'll play

the music for them, tell them it's the same sound
my blood makes going through my ears, hoping
they'll listen long enough to understand

before one of them asks me to shut off the noise,
or to put on something with words in it,
before I'll have to tell them it's the words
that mess things up sometimes.

L'avalasse

The old women of our parish
say such rain, *l'avalasse*,
throws sheets of sleep across your house
to wash away whatever burden
the day has brought. They walk outside
in their nightgowns as soon as the bullfrogs
stiffen in the ditch and hunker down,
believing the water will cleanse them of aches
and lighten the weight
their years have built.

It's enough for me to step to the porch
with the dog to watch the backyard fill.
Inside, my wife and boys draw close
and breathe with such peace the house almost glows.
Their sleep is thick and well-deserved.
There's nothing worth waking them for
as long as this storm holds us to its heart.
I know the dreams they share will be enough
to keep us afloat when morning comes.

Outside, a murder of crows has landed,
pecking its way through the mess this rain
has washed off our house into the grass.
Somewhere, the old women are bathing,
their lesson in the water coming down—
no matter how it pounds, this rain
will not outlast Noah's. Our land
is thirstier than his, our sins
much easier to wash away.

Come Rain or Come Shine

This is a promise without boundary or sense
until the first night the baby wakes
every hour with a pain in his voice
that can only be soothed by his mother's breath
on his neck or the soft comfort of her rocking
from foot to foot in the dark; until days pass
without a single conversation about anything
except the baby's fever or sore mouth
or his eating or not eating or smiling or not smiling;
until sleep and quiet are your only desires.

And then comes the rainy morning when the baby sleeps
past nine, or the night he goes to sleep before ten;
when the bed is warm and touch is no dream
but something shared like a hot, slow-cooked meal
unrushed by crying or need; or that long moment
when a wife steps from the bath and is not mother
but a clenching in your chest that makes the day shine
enough for everyone in the house; and suddenly you know
the distance between the beginning of these words
and the blessing of love that will help you carry them out.

The Maple Leaf Bar

At the Maple Leaf Bar
in uptown New Orleans
a few doors from Jacquimo's
on Oak off Carrolton
the pretty bar maid, Rachel,
pops Orville Redenbacher
into the microwave.

Three weeks after the flood
a customer, a neighborhood regular,
brought the cases of popcorn
looted from Walmart.
No use at his house
without power,
but with rain leaking
through blue plastic tarps.
A sweet gum tree leans against
his collapsed front porch.

The insurance company
won't talk to him anymore,
except to argue
whether it was wind or water:
whichever pays less.

We drink cold beer
from Abita Springs
across Lake Ponchartrain.
Rachel tears open the bag
and passes around the hot kernels
to the small crowd.

The mad-woman-wind,
rude and loud,
lusty and mean,
is now Maple Leaf gossip,
but not even Katrina
is so ill a wind
to blow no good.

We all agree
the popcorn is the best
we've ever had.

GLENN J. BERGERON II

Grand Isle 1996

The clouds this night collapse with violence
Into themselves, the frothing Gulf their score,
Then rise to forge a new design, each tense
With struggle to hold form, impermanence

Their constant state. Below, the fitful shore
Endeavors to maintain a faithful line,
Establishing frail boundaries once more,
Demanding less than what it sought before.

My last night on Grand Isle, I face the brine
Of maddened crests, each salted sting the shard
Of some Great Sculptor chipping to define
From blemished stone his grandiose design.

Silent Retreat: Grand Coteau, Louisiana

> *You followed to a stone,*
> *And there the trail was lost.*
> —Yvor Winters

With morning prayer fulfilled, I kneel beneath
A dampened oak to brush away a wreath
Of moss from lichened stone. Two names appear:
Deceased from Mother's side. Nervous, I peer
Beyond the lilting rows of buckled tombs
Toward the seminary's waking rooms
As if communing with the dead will break
My weekend pledge of silence, and for my sake,
The aging priests would have me start again.
My reason soon takes hold and I begin
The normal things I figure people say:
"What were you like?" and "Will we meet someday?"
Then wonder if they know you're there or do
Such visits count beyond appeasing you?
Is it indeed all bosh? Am I the source
Inventing for myself a fool's discourse?
The silence deepens. Selfish questions cease
And I decide to leave the dead in peace.

JOHN BIGUENET

Scrimshaw

Something like a sigh, like the flutter of nuns
climbing a stone staircase or wings
flapping against velvet curtains,
something spoken beyond the echoes
of an ear's arched corridors,
the musculature of air,
falling in the trembling octaves of the felt,
something that silenced us so abruptly
we turned and looked at one another.
What had gone forth from us as words
returned as stillness, ripples of a solitude
not among the chemicals of our memories.
Had something died? It was seconds, centuries
before our murmuring began again.

As if the universe had flickered, as if
the great falls of Time spilling the deafening present
into the bottomless pool of the past
had ceased—even the electrons of the Himalayas
paused in their circuits, and those huge rocks fell
from existence, forgotten angels of an unconscious Motion,
they were disappearing they were being born
they had never been they were suffering
the first death, and we with them—
and immediately (how else to describe an eternity)
began again. That first instant,
discontiguous with the instant before,
was horribly uncomfortable. But with the first few words,
we reinvented our lives.

This new age was beyond us. All things
seemed altered, seemed to waver with the new heat
that infused them. As if we inhabited
buildings whose narrow foundations had powdered
and blown into the streets under the mountainous weight.
In the hesitation before collapse,
while millions of disrupted stones
clung to their idea of the building they had been,
the skyscraper hung in the air, teetering

above the habit of its crushed foundation.
The swirling dust glazed our clay eyes.
We waited beneath a canopy of winter light
for our towers to decline,
to crumble into themselves like stars.
We savored the luxury of unequaled spectacle
accorded the victims of unimaginable disaster.
We were being honored in the same fashion
as a man drawn across the membrane of a black hole
or a woman devoured by a minotaur.
But by dark it became clear that we might as well
go inside, for the hesitation persisted
and the snow was scalding our faces.
There was memory in the mortar;
things were holding on. In our own way,
we were proud of our floating cities.
But no one ever mentioned the twelve inches of light
emptying into the room at the base of its walls.

And yet, most do not notice. Or else
they have no word for it, and so say nothing.
I have tried to open their eyes,
but they are impatient with my metaphors.
Still, even in this new tapestry, a raveling.
A wisp of thread and the full weight bearing down
on the flaw. In the imperceptible collapse of silk,
years stagger. Finally the conclusion of simple forces:
a wound running across the fabric
like the wave splayed by a fin,
making a sound something like a sigh,
something like a man scratching his story in bone
in the interior of this whale.

Nine Nudes

A woman awakes from a dream, remembering nothing
in particular, perhaps only a sense of shadows
coalescing just under the surface of pale water.
Unable to sleep, she watches herself with pleasure:
in the shifting darkness of the bedroom mirror,
everything seems to be moving around her body.

Or two women wake from dreamless sleep, each body
curling into the other, each mouth reciting nothing
but the sour taste of salt. Each face, a mirror
of polished stone, lustrous among the fringed shadows
that spill like pillows about their heads, as vague pleasure
begins to stiffen like darkness thickening into water.

Or a girl undresses and steps into dark water.
A breeze riffles the reflection of her sand-colored body.
Chilled, she leans into her shape. A sigh of pleasure
rises like a bubble toward her ear, yet she hears nothing
but her own pulse. In her hands, she cups small shadows
as small feet shatter the surface of the dark mirror.

Or a boy, bathing, studies himself in the mirror
and finds a companion standing in shallow water.
The steaming room decays into dust and shadows
as he regards the image of his naked body.
The knot that tightens between its legs has nothing
to do with his trembling fingers, those shards of pleasure.

Or a man and a woman, embracing in passionless pleasure,
mistake the act of love for crawling on a mirror.
Closing their eyes on each other, they want nothing
but to lose themselves like ice melting in water.
As if asleep, each dreams of a coldly luminescent body
motionless beneath the fresco of its flailing shadows.

Or a woman rises from bed, fumbling in the shadows
for light. Her flesh still carries an impression of pleasure
like the sheets still describing his suddenly absent body.
She stands before the shut door as if it were a mirror.
The polished wood reminds her of blond water
and repeats to her the whole story, but explains nothing.

Or you, a cloud of shadows drifting in a mirror,
think of the pleasure of sinking in warm water,
of a naked body becoming nothing.

The Wall Behind the Mirror

Text

The lightbulb looks like a pear
if one is willing to forget
what a pear looks like.

And the chandelier of fruit
swaying beneath banana leaves
reminds one of incandescent light.

Homily

Can there be more to metaphor
than imprecise remembering?
Another kind of poem exists,

immaculately stupid,
swallowing the names of things
in favor of their silences.

Exhortation

Take a lesson from your child:
stuff your mouth with your fingers.

JOHN BLAIR

Oleander

In 1967, in Cartersville, Georgia
a drunk flew his car into the open arms
of the girl who lived next door to us,

his Buick blowing through her
like a squall. She was sixteen,
walking home with someone else's

six-year-old son. At the last
thin instant she heaved the kid
like a stone into a weedy ditch.

What I wonder now is how
he must have felt, that boy,
finding himself alone, cradled

in the stiff winter mud, remembering
that girl, so quick, who had pitched
him away forever.

Lao Tse wrote that eternity
is the return to destiny,
which is the salt and clay and sky, which is

the fluid arc of what has been, forever
becoming us: maybe I was that boy in the ditch,
maybe I lay there in the mist

with the gray light of morning cool
on my face and listened to the car engine
ticking like a locust

as it cooled, waiting for a reason to move,
smelling burned rubber and weeds,
antifreeze, roadside oleander

with its poisonous flowers broad
as magnolia blossoms. Maybe I could hear
the tiny sounds of insects fingering through the debris

like haruspices looking for reasons and so
I understood all at once what the world intended
with its oleander bitter as death

or the things unsaid or the hard
pavement of roads
running away from us endlessly,

how we stand up from the mud to wait for it,
arms flung wide, braced for whatever might be coming,
whatever's already here.

Winter Storm, New Orleans

If it could, the earth would wash
you and all of us from her as a lover

washes away experience. Winter, even here,
is the shudder of flesh touched by foulness.

The mud pulls at your feet
like sorrow. If you try, you can even find

comfort in the dead smell of coat leather;
for a moment the wind is the voice of grief,

slashes inward with a fistful of cold rain,
then dissolves too into insensible drizzle.

The idea of snow is wrong here.
So you watch for it,

the random lights dropping
new through the trees, Yankee

whiteness to change your life.
The wind stumbles across the street

and is gone. The city settles
like the weathered ruin it always was.

The Dogs of Grass

*Heaven and Earth do not act from kindnesss;
they deal with all things as dogs of grass.*
—Lao Tse

The dogs brighten with every
subtle degree of desiccation, left
to the cool settling of the wind
as it finds its better self down low.

She moves, word upon word,
through the grass and bones
of her expectations, little grub
who knows more than she ever

wanted to know, how nothing
down here can much matter, where
the mud is frozen and hard
and cuts with its wimpled edges

the flesh. Blessed are the meek,
the down-to-earth, the laid-low.
None of this is really about her,
and never was, girl who wants

too much, who wants God's gentle
hand and a little luck. The dull
layers of shame and avarice accrete
like varnish, yellow against

the white of bone and the calm
glow of winter grass. The skin
of the world is ice and slick enough
to slide you right out of it,

if there's someone to push hard enough.
There you go, pretty girl, bye-bye,
and she crawls away through
the stubble and the worm cast

to no possible other-where,
bloodied and helpless and living
on the thin grace of sonnets
and sweat. Holy girl, stumble Mary,

arms full of grimness and light.
Creep away, run away, fly away home,
become the field beneath you planted
in grief, become the dogs of grass

that do not reap nor sow nor care, but lie
fulfilled in the careless rain.

BEAU BOUDREAUX

Drifting Off, East North East

I'm the one
inside the crowded bistro

reading alone
with an untouched martini

a young woman in floral dress
pedals by

and there's a boy cross-legged
at the trolley stop fumbling papers

why close the sculpture garden at night . . .
I've never been to Boston

Baltimore or Philly—
the window, people sip

outside the coffeeshop
form a patio

may be too much
with myself

like a cheap shot
of tequila after many rounds with friends

is not last year, but a decade
when I sat for the first time

through a matinee
sunshine cooking car seats

a shock sitting into
like biting a lemon.

On Bayou Sauvage

Martins dive from my memory
and into their nest in the rafters
of the boat shed.

Old men fish on the wharves,
telling lies to themselves
and each other.

In August, mosquitoes and gnats
come in clouds
from the rozo cane
along Bayou Sauvage.
Gulls and hawks climb
to their apex of sky.
Scores of mullet swim
below osprey and fish crows.

Barges putter by, heading to Lake Borgne,
Lake Catherine, and the Gulf of Mexico,
their waves jostling
the water lilies.

For a moment, the water is still
and a voice calls from the cane.
With a clam shell, on a dusty culvert,
I'm trying to write my name
which no one has taught me to spell.

Slides of a Life in Blue Air

1.

Here, the boy Lucius plays
with armadillo bones
beside a dry ditch.

2.

Here he is along Highway 36,
up toward Abita Springs,
flying a kite on a field
charred by snipe hunters.
All day, he flew the kite alone,
at the edge of the field,
wishing he were someone else
in another time.

3.

Was he fishing
in this scum-filled pond,
or was he
merely imagining?

4.

What about here? The night he heard
John Lennon had been shot dead?
For a month he couldn't speak,
and a priest performed an exorcism.
The parents, as always, were oblivious
to his spirit.

5.

Here's that time he rode his bike
from LaCombe to Talisheek
to fight a bully,
a distance of some twenty miles,
then collapsed when the first punch was thrown.

6.

Here it's 1982, and all the fields
are dead from summer.
He's walking and thinking
about the Great White North,
about Canada
and all the ducks
he shoots in winter.
That same summer,
in a different landscape,
he's jumping from skiff to skiff
at his grandmother's place
on Bayou Sauvage.
He's looking for crabs
under the floorboards of the skiffs,
and for dark fish in the wells.

7.

Here he is at fifteen in Slidell, Louisiana,
dying of pneumonia
in his father's house,
as a fever kills day by day,
leaving only the charred fields
and empty lagoons.

Light Theology and the Persimmon Tree

for Dorothy Bourque Miller

Her kitchen was not filled with ordinary light;
it was the one selected room she made all hers.
From the north window above her sink she gazed
at the white tailed kites hovering over the ponds,
listened idly to noisy killdeers chattering through
the lazy afternoons in the pasture all summer long.
When she was not satisfied with the lovely things
she could bring us to, she thought selectively about
the fruited hedgerows and orchards this time of year.
Mayhaw jellies and muscadine jams were but some
bright possibilities, but they never passed the test.

Between the *Charadrius vociferus* in the pasture
and that north window was a persimmon tree.
When the skins on the fruit were just beginning
to put on a lemon sheen, she would begin to see
the red-gold they would become. She waited
for the first frost to begin to relax the branches'
hold and for the fruit to go into the manufacture
of the final sugaring before she wrapped each
globe in crisp white tissue. As the year parceled
out its dwindling light, she came to our back doors
before dawn, left us shallow boxes of golden suns.

Scratch

Since that afternoon years ago
when my mother put us on our knees
and told us she was leaving,
I have placed myself in the world,
measured myself against the horizon,
let the sky cover me like some angel bird
hovering. I have seen wide ribbons
of pine making a trot-line at the earth's edge.
I have studied things up-close: stunted trees
growing out of rock. I have gone beyond
tree lines where grasses open seedpods
like prayers. I have stood at the water's
edge and wobbled, and still no one
knows who knifed the unreadable lettering
on my mother's new cedar chifferobe
that day. She and my father drove to town
to buy garfish for our usual Friday supper
at my aunt's house. We were questioned again
on her return but no one confessed—through
the fish cleaning, the seasoning, the frying.
I can't remember when exactly we laughed
and ran through the yard with our cousins.
It was night when we went home. We were happy.
Just last week, some fifty years later,
one of us brings it up in my mother's
presence. She has not walked for years
and it is no big matter to her now,
but none of us are fessing up today either.
We all know who didn't do it,
and one of us knows who did.

The Black Door in *Arnaudville*

for Gloria Fiero

It might be what you don't see that most pleases
in this scene. There are possible banks everywhere
in this thick expanse of lively grassland. Water teases
a presence here and storms embed themselves in the charged air.

Beyond the darkest trees on the horizon whole families
may be filling sacks with choupique or handfishing for turtles.
Lovers could settle in away from us in that little cluster of trees

near the barn. But these are passing things. They startle
no one, mere skitterings to circumvent the black door of mysteries
opening the rusty tin-covered, white pyramid amidst all the marbled

life teeming here, a grave opening defying opening. No one sees
anything discernible beyond this dark plane. There is something there
we think or hope, but it invites nothing we can easily take comfort in, frees
nothing. Yet, it is the painter's gift to us, something the landscape has to bear.

ANN REISFELD BOUTTÉ

My Mother's Suitcase

Unlike its pristine,
wheeled descendants
for sale on
department store shelves,
it suggests a history
of adventures past.
Rectangular lines,
now bowed, reflect
her chronic over packing.
Nylon in a shade of taupe,
it's streaked and soiled
from trans-world travels.
Once shining hardware
is scratched and tarnished.
It touched down
in capitals of Europe—
Paris, London, Rome,
withstood exotic lands—
Iran, Iraq, Afghanistan,
survived Antarctica,
Earth's nethermost region.

Months after her
last hospitalization,
it rests in my bedroom,
the contents neatly folded,
reminding of her stories
I long to hear again.

Walker Evans

In order to develop something akin to miracle,
he acquired a taste for the peeling billboards

that used to promise sweetness to every man
on the day and night crews at Chicago Steel.

He had an eye for the architecture of failure:
the straw broom at an angle in the immaculate

corner of a dirt-floored, single-room shack
housing generations of sharecropper families.

He praised the perfection in the ordinary,
in "famous men" with barefoot children

lining the edge of a tilled field outside Decatur
or in black Chryslers along an endless avenue.

From the alignment of light with shadow,
he chiseled away a new and affluent language

hidden in the columns at Belle Grove Plantation.
Evans spoke of how the past can shape the future

and negotiated, for us, the cracks in Alabama clay
like the Pangaea breaking into singular worlds.

Flight Theory

The barn swallow knew
       all of her eggs
but one
              would be obliterated.
After death, when one of her talons
was carried into the fire ants' den,
that swallow lived again.
                    Certain consolation
spells agony. Just ask the Puritans.
Such was not the case
   for a hummingbird
that blundered into particle board
newly raised in its flight path. . .
stiletto beak
impaled inches deep.
For the Museum of Natural History and Wildlife,
workers jig-sawed around the limp body.
Everywhere
              the same story spreads
its wings.
I'm talking about the police chief
shooting down a heron.
                    Right there
at Main and 1st.
That was Grandview I think.
Or Prosser. *Could have been*
anywhere.
              It was something to do.
Something for small town humdrum.

Locals argued
                    which special interest group
would be first
                    to take offense.
I'm talking about the gulls and crows
wheeling above a tractor
ousting nightcrawlers and gophers
into the open. The birds dove
    and swallowed,
their shitting so bad
the farmer constructed a flail:
a broomstick with baling wire
did the trick.
                    You wouldn't believe
such hardship. A woman I loved once
loved me the way girls want horses.
It's true
    but not what I'm saying here.
Naw, not quite.
I'm talking about seasons
of owls smothered in the granary.
Bet there's more to that story, eh?
Can't drive through the countryside
without dead crows dangling from fence wire.
Be clever: Say murder. Say it!
Tonight's sunset like the sheen
on John James Audubon's
                            dissection table.
Ha! More like love spread-eagled against a wall.
An evening full of starlings
pouring through the air like unchecked water.
I held her and we witnessed,
                            still no closer
to comprehension.
How many nights did I try
to retrace the complexities
of starlings with my hands over her skin?
I've double-checked the pica and font.
I've got my theories.
            Story of cruelty
without meaning,
how is it you always insinuate
yourself among these syllables?
Audubon killed what he loved best.
Come on, don't look so

surprised. A story has to start somewhere.
I'm told on his mantel Vermeer
kept a flute
                carved from a swan's wing bone.
Nothing knows the wing like wind.
Let's pretend the first angel
throttled a white swan for its wings
and its nest
                in our hearts.
Tell them Wm. Blake sketched his wife
and sang to her for an hour
then dropped dead and that's a fact.
Dear metaphor,
let down your hair for me,
put on your black silk,
your best
                "come hither."
Don't fail to fall off the tongue.
Beautiful. God! Yes!
                        Fruit is bound to rot
and flies descend.
Wave them off,
                they return.
Persistent as sperm.
I'm talking about that summer
the syllables,
                multitudes of them,
darkened the sky above us.
If I ever see her again,
                        I'll speak
of pebbles transported south
in the crops of a million birds.
Tell them, will you?
Okay, okay. A feather rests
on my windowsill
and when the baseboard heater
kicks on as I write this,
that feather dances
                a little.

63

CATHARINE SAVAGE BROSMAN

Tree in Winter

In frozen gestures—sculpted, fixed in place—
the maple tree, now leafless, stark, and blind,
devises, from its denudation, grace,
its seven limbs uplifted, arched, entwined;

like Shiva, who destroys and then creates—
the master of the universal dance,
a constant tourbillon, the round of fates,
disposing newly of the stuff of chance.

The tree's deep being orders the design
of root and trunk—no alien intent—
well replicated in each texture, line,
and leaf—implicit as the branch is bent.

And thus, in its intensity of fact,
it carries promise—sap run, dress of green—
its visions wedded in the verdant act
of opening its eye-buds, proud, serene.

Fire in the Mind

Among a stack of old spring binders filled
with notes—the trophies, or the detritus,
of forty years of teaching, taken home
like ashes from a crematorium—
this jewel, not mine: a senior thesis, bound,
from nineteen sixty-two, done by a girl
who'd learned sufficient French in just four years
to write so well, with such authority,

that, as I leaf through now, I am amazed.
She wrote on Simone de Beauvoir. Our minds
met easily, and in her prose my hand
is sometimes visible—the mentor's genes.
She also was a darling of her class,
the Queen of Rondelet, a "Beauty," rich
in flair, charm, wit. She even cooked. Two men
who both became Rhodes Scholars courted her,

but they went off to Oxford, while she took
her doctorate in history, then left
for Paris, favored *haute couture*, and did
translation. Once we lunched al fresco, near
the Louvre—friends still, in the prime of life—
but spoke of trivial things. She later wed
in his château a wealthy Frenchman, not
an intellectual, and smoked herself

to death. She's buried in the family vault
in Père-Lachaise. A close friend tried to find
the grave, but wandered vainly in that maze,
a honeycomb, until she heard a voice
instructing her to leave: "Go buy yourself
a bottle of expensive French perfume,
in memory of me." —Forever gone,
long evenings spading in the library,

the thrilling mastery of that new tongue,
the hunt for ignis fatuus, happiness,
elusive always; gone that perfect sphere
of consciousness, a bubble, full—delight
and disaffection, laughter, cough. What I
inherit are these words in carbon black,
as on a cavern wall, the signs that speak
of winged illusions, fire in the mind.

Envoi

Dear Mary Ann, your old professor says:
Work diligently there in Père-Lachaise.
You see things better from the other shore,
as mortal matters give concern no more.
You can't be interrupted in the tomb
when studying the cryptic book of doom;
distractions must be few, and time permits
the leisured application of your wits.
You'll reach a new perfection in your style,
observe the human comedy the while,
and see things pass that we cannot yet see,
the very spirit of all history.

On the Bayou

The birds are bright as paradise at noon:
blue herons, cormorants, pink ibis, gulls.
With slapping sounds, two muskrats slip away
behind our wake. Some driftwood moves, alive,
and paddles near; a creature on the bank

begins to lumber down. The beasts make dull
officiants, half in hibernation still,
but hungry. Someone throws a fish among
the ripples; in a shine of hide, a flash
of teeth, the fish and alligator both

are gone. We float among dark eddies, bits
of spring debris, and silence. Farther back,
the thick, tenebrous recesses of swamp
inscribe a revery, the Spanish moss
and branches dangling in oneiric shapes,

the palms more beautiful than dreams. The light,
pale fingers through the cypress, and the wind
release the evening, and we leave, confirmed
in being, as it were by sacrament—
a body sacrificed, a flesh remade.

STEVEN C. BROWN, JR.

Wormlight

At seven, I wondered
if God could sleep,
his belly flecked
with fields of wormlight.

My parents slept below,
nuzzled in June's oven,
dreaming their meaty dreams.

And the river, rheumy
as a kid's sick eye,
watched them sleep
and would not flow.

An owl gagged
on something hatched.
A green anole
grew lovely in the throat
and struck its skull
against the windowpane

as if to say, *No one sleeps,*
no one sleeps
and no one dreams entirely

which is the law
of worms weaving lightning
in the dark, and all those born
beneath the open claw.

July's Entomology

July's insect sun, its hive above the yard
drips its blinding sugars on our tongues.
The kids are strung along the leaves, cocoons
of so little memory but what is shared
by the maple's limb, that red festoon
of birds, those frogs of *sturm und drang*—

becoming what the senses always urged,
what they always meant by *being*. This span
of trees with loose follicles of leaf, the star
of synapse where sight and knowledge merge
into one upheaval of the dead's desire:

What could it possibly mean other than
the magi's return to light-imbibing fields
where grows the germ and mystery of faith?

And if not a christ, then the hive's collective arm—
something giant that finds us in its world,
not as strangers, but as daughters of the worm,
a tongue unwhorled from the butterfly's mouth.

Animalia

After the splintering rains of January
and overflow of rice fields,
after the gorged gutters and watersheds
purge into the city streets,
the mice move their loose militias
into the mobile homes
like the plague-tooth of Yahweh.

It does not help: the sticky traps,
the snaps and poison logs.
They die in the walls and smell
of mango rot and papermills.
It is their way of staying.

If we pried the paneling
off the frame, what a spill of bone,
of brittle relics, of spine like prayer beads
fit for an infant's wrist.

At night, we listen
to the matchstick-scratching
above the lamp and armoire.
If it is prayer, it is against us,
against the soap and cold milk,
the white rose in a vase.
It is unto the wood itself
to cave like Jericho,
a familiar prayer: to get inside,
to get their way.

ELIZABETH BURK

Learning to Love Louisiana

"Where are the mountains?"
I ask, after an hour's drive
through flat-filled landscapes
of sugar cane and rice fields, miles
without trees, unprotected from open sky.

Elemore calls it the prairie;
the name blows wide open
the shut down, frightened spaces
in my heart,

transforms this stripped bare
boggy land into primal frontier—
grand vistas of grassy earth
framed by cloudscapes,

dotted with tin shacks, trailers
huddled like hitchhikers
by the side of the road,

the lackadaisical towns, windows boarded,
looking in daytime as though they were
shut down for the night,

the gray mist's endless drizzle
filling the swamps, marshes, basins
to the brim.

Why not surrender, succumb, languish
at the edge of a rice field, watching
the wind sway the marshy grasses

out here on the prairie,
so close to god,
where there is no place to hide?

My Husband's Visit

Home from work, I find him
in the kitchen chopping onions, celery,
dicing peppers. Peeled parboiled tomatoes
sit naked on the cutting board
dripping juice and seeds. I inhale

the aromas of garlic, thyme, white wine
poured Julia Child style, one dollop
for the stew, one slurp for the cook,
before he spoons into my mouth
a roux rich and redolent with spice.

Come back to Louisiana, babe, he says,
putting into my still-open mouth
a plump piece of hot sausage,
my mouth that is always open for more,
and I'll cook for you forever.

And I want to, I do, I want that hound dog
in the back seat of our pickup, head poking
out the window, ears flapping in the breeze,
the chanky-chank music blaring on the radio
as we drive over bumpy back roads to town

but I'm a set-in-stone city girl
raised by skyscrapers, wary
of wide open spaces, afraid my life
will be cast adrift, a pirogue lost
in the tall marshy reeds, empty

as the galaxy of wine bottles he leaves
behind on the kitchen floor where
papery garlic skins lie scattered,
still curled as if around the body
of the clove no longer there.

71

The Bride of Quietness

My husband, when he was my husband, possessed
electrifying energy, humor,
the vital heat of violent force compressed. . .
contraries in a controlling frame. Few more

creative and compelling men could fire
the clay I scarcely dared to call my soul.
Shapeless, lacking properties of higher
existence, it was perfect for the mold

he cast me in: classic receptacle,
a thing for use but full of elegance,
an ode to Greece, forever practical,
tellingly patterned with the hunt and dance.

My lines were lies; and yet he seemed to see
aesthetic validation in my form.
I asked him not to draw away from me.
He said he feared he might commit some harm—

some accidental, inadvertent hurt—
and shatter in an instant all the love
he'd poured out in the effort to convert
my ordinary mind to a work of

art. And how he shuddered if I assumed
a new position or a point of view!
As if I were a royal vase entombed
after the ancient style, and the issue

of my movement could only be a change
in where he stood, relative to his wife.
I must perdure inanimate and strange
and still, if he would justify his life.

For I was the object of his most profound
research, the crafty subject of his thesis,
and all I had to do to bring him down
was let my heart break into all those pieces

it ached to break into in any case.
Upon his graduation, when the guests
had gone, and night was settling on his face,
raising my voice above his dreams I confessed

that beauty held no truth for me, nor truth
beauty, but I was made as much of earth
as I had been, barbaric and uncouth,
enjoined to rhythm, shiftings, blood and birth,

and void of principle. He said he'd father
no children. I could hardly help knowing
that he'd be wrong to trust me any farther.
By sunrise it was clear he would be going

soon. Now from time to time I see him here
and there. The shoulders have gone slack, the eyes
conduct a lesser current and I fear
that when they catch me spying, it's no surprise

to him. He always found poetic justice
amusing, and he knows I wait my turn.
The artist dies; but what he wrought will last
forever, when I cradle his cold ashes in this urn.

Sharks

". . .[A]ll angel is not'ing more than the shark well goberned."
—Old Fleece in Moby-Dick

You have to keep them under close watch.
They attack without warning, sudden as a squall,
underslung jaws swinging loose on the gilled latch

like a baby getting ready to bawl
its head off. Treading time, they circle the soul
survivor, never doubting he'll fall

from grace soon enough, dizzied by their sunlit shoal.
Light yaws and tacks, blown back against his battered vision
by the wind their fins wake. Whole

days drift by, like seaweed. Though history seems to shun
him, and sunburn raises blisters on his mouth,
he sucks salt from the Pacific Ocean

as a baby pulls a breast. Sharks swim south
of Paradise, around the Cape of Sin,
but he who clings like a barnacle to the lessons of his youth

earns the salute of a scaly fin.
He may yet teach a school of hammerheads
to dance on the head of a pin.

Two Roses

She is an angel in rose
Etched on a November sky.
He is a rose—
They are two roses, burning brightly.

They kiss in the car,
Their lips like petals: pink.
They must drive far
To find God, I think.

I think that angels' wings spread
Against the sky are red
As roses, and fly not at all.
They fall

And fall, flower-flames,
And as they fall, they love and kiss,
Calling each other's cherished name.
God loves this.

God loves this—
The twining, the arc.
They fall together,
Lightly, into the winter dark.

WILLIAM BEDFORD CLARK

"Katrina refugees return—weigh future"

The photo, widely syndicated, shows
A woman and son, their midcity home
Awash in sludge, intent upon saving some
Long boxy thing. A teak armoire? Who knows?

It's Chan for sure (you can and do see that),
No matronly *maman* you're pleased to say,
Bird-boned and delicate as on the day
She split—and bruised your mind, but fed the cat.

Decades ago, you wished her ill, and yet
Had hardly asked for this: Those gulag eyes
Have left off questioning. Beyond surprise
She does what hands can do, takes what she'll get.

If curses work, then benediction stands a chance:
Dread Lord, bless mother, son, and all new mendicants.

CARLOS COLÓN

His Last Letter

for Dietrich Bonhoeffer

his last letter to Maria
was never received
there was a different guard
on duty that day
that Christmas day
this new fellow
softhearted
like the regular guard
smuggled the letter out
just like the others
stopping briefly outside
the compound to move thin
fingers across Dietrich's
most private thoughts
mouthing each word

later right before
the letter was posted
a black glove grabbed
the guard's shoulder
another ripped the letter
from his inside pocket
the new guard was
shot in the street
the old guard
reassigned

in a chuckling moment
it was decided to mail
the envelope to Maria
who upon opening it
would discover
only ashes

but even at that
the envelope never
reached its destination

though the words
she never saw
remained with Dietrich
accompanied him
up the steps
toward death
toward his own
resurrection

Refracted Memory

Rambunctious, headstrong,
my three-year-old brother Rick
runs off the diving board
into the family pool.

I still see him flailing,
hear him wailing for help.
I still feel the coolness, as I clutch
the metal ladder nearby, while my dad
from nowhere apparent finally
snatches him to safety.

Thirty years later,
Dad and Rick have
a different recollection.
Dad remembers Rick
paddling "like a puppy"
across the pool.
Rick's memory,
presumably colored by my father's,
envisions the same scene.

Yet the nightmares continue.
The unexpected splash.
The strident screams.
Am I terrified,
or just petrified
by jealousy?
Do I pretend not to hear
the screams, or have they
disappeared beneath the waves?
My throat, my eyes, my grip
tighter, tighter, tighter.

Foragers

Gagging, bent double from the dumpster's stench
I've come to add my small donation to,
I catch these two I haven't seen in weeks,
not since the hurricane swept through and left
these, the survivors of life on the street
slumming sometimes in my poor neighborhood.

The guy lifts a flask as if in salute;
his girlfriend, stoned already, just looks down.
They've found a home, abandoned gas station
where they can sleep inside its looted store,
forage a dinner from overlooked stuff,
the junk food only junkies can keep down.

I don't want intimacy but I smile.
Today they won't ask: What would I give them?
My food comes from the Salvation Army.
Theirs could, too, if they got in line with me.
I think they won't. It's for the families
along our street sans electricity.
This pair knows survival tactics I can't use.

To Christ Our Lord

September 2, 2005

This tiny corner of the fallen world
given to me that I can keep in place,
the North where it first meets the broken East,
site of the sun, staggering to raise its head:
this, I say, is the world of after-flood.

The hurricane passed over New Orleans.
No one foresaw the toll its wake could make,
the graves disgorging bodies, the new dead
fallen from rooftops where they sought refuge,
the looters with their only chance at bread.

Obviously, some great lesson is at hand,
Christ, which has escaped me yet. Rush it here.
I need to find that something in the sun
I know is there, even if it's pale fire,
the sun I've made a symbol of your grace—

Was I wrong there? A symbol of your face
hidden from us. The looters pass my house
where I am walled in; they carry water.
I have little. Should I ask them for some?
Is this my lesson, morning of white sun?

Downtown

In another world, when I was little,
when my feet on the car seat didn't reach
the floor even, but I could see outside,
downtown Detroit was Rome or Istanbul,
Constantinople when I heard the word.

My mother wore gloves and hat, her veil black,
the elevator operator wore gloves
at Hudson's Department Store, Santa Claus
wore gloves and Mickey Mouse and Minnie, too,
in the movie at the Cass Theater
where the ceiling's pink, naked cherubim
staring down made me think of Porky Pig.
Outside the theater in that bronze light
memory casts, the organ grinder, monkey
with silver cup. I gave him a penny.

This was my downtown after World War II.
But reminiscence is not literature.
I come to this page shaking as I write.
I'm home, I'm calm, downtown New Orleans
fifteen minutes and this cup of mint tea
away. You know, they're all the same, downtowns.
This is the third millennium of the poor
who smell, who talk funny, who sell the drugs
your friends depend on for their sustenance.
I won't describe downtown. You know downtown.
I just wanted to record what I saw.
He was there; he looked just like one of them,
moving among the crowd, doing what he does.
Except for the palms I wouldn't have known
something was going on. The nail holes, blood.
I came home. I don't do well with miracle.

SIDNEY MCCALLUM CREAGHAN

Dark Nights of Unbridled Color

He exchanged his ear to save his heart.
Danced for months to no music.

His hands became burnt offerings
of tiny beds, irises and red chairs.

Haystacks unbridled into fierce midnights
and the skies whirled desires blue.

Yellow stars fell like mania and salt.
He lost his shoes. He lost his shirt.

Azure labored like a loyal friend
to undergird a generous mind.

But soon the secrets of lavender and gold
goaded him beyond his tether. One day

in a field of unprecedented green
a single horse of unsaddled beauty

undid him, sent him chasing his own gods.
He raced so far away

he painted himself to sleep.

KEVIN CUTRER

Lord's Own Anointed

If Henry Hebert seems a little off
it's due to the fact he was whopped upside
the head by Harley Swearinger's 2 x 4
one afternoon ten years ago outside
the mower shop when he had made a joke
about the woman Harley lived in sin with.
They say his eyes went bugged and bright before
his knees collapsed and he fell on his face.
Never the same, they say. Not ever the same.

Lost his job, lost his stitches, got the Spirit.
You see him in his short necktie, suspenders
holding them awful pinstriped pants up high,
his belly like a baby's poking out,
out by the hardware store, by the old highway,
holding his imitation-leather bible,
grinning his one-gold-toothed, immaculate grin.
He stands out there to greet the customers,
not hired nor shooed away by management.

He talks a funny way I can't describe,
not that he ever talks that much at all
but mostly stands around and grins at you.
They warn of idle hands, but idle tongues
are just as bad, ask Henry Hebert why.
He's the most thoughtful-speaking man you'll meet
in this or any town, if he will say
a word or two about the holy scriptures.
The preacher calls on him to pray each Sunday,

and every time he has a different prayer
more blessed than any message that young pastor
with all his years at college could invent.
It's never rambling, or too rushed on through,
but sentence after sentence simply sings.
He prays with all the energy a workingman
puts to his pillow every night to sleep,
that hard-won peace that only comes from struggle.
He seems a little off but, child, he's on.

82

On Dale's Role in the Christmas Pageant

You're asking him, a man who had to learn
to talk again after his head was split
from falling off the tailgate of a truck,
his first successful word a high-pitched *shit!*
in a hospital bed surrounded by each branch
of our sprawling live oak of a family tree,
you're asking that man there to put more love
in his voice, portraying Joseph in the manger?
Preacher, let's talk about the Dale I know.

This is a man who, on our wedding night,
was asleep by nine to wake at four for milking.
I've watched him, morning after faithful morning,
cuss at the local news, mouth full of grits,
and turn in, nine on the dot, every night,
for twenty years; have heard him cough and yell
through mortgage payments, diaper changes, love—
he is a loving man, I know for sure,
but, Reverend, his voice don't rise like yours or mine.

You've heard him in the mismatched harmonies
the congregation gives the Lord on Sundays,
his nails-on-slate apart from men and ladies,
moaning the hymns, a humble shepherd crying
with the angelic choir surpassing him.
It may not be the melody that's written,
and maybe I am not the one to judge,
but you can't say he doesn't get the message.
His music comes from somewhere else than sound.

It's the same dry crackle like a wheel on gravel
whether he's crooning with his Conway Twitty
or getting on to Jed for breaking curfew.
You tell me, does a bear not feel the same
for her small cubs, grunting and bellowing,
as momma birds filling the trees with song?
My Dale's a man who grinds his words like grain;
Samson himself is pushing a stone wheel
inside his throat: so what he says, he means.

Butcher

I will not die asleep in bed.
I'm likelier to kick and squeal
like those two hogs I killed today
come crowding up the holding pen
together, nervous from the prod.
I am the one that had to wait
after the bullet stunned the other,
the one that had to listen
as skin whopped and swathed the wet,
hard killing floor, until next shot.
They writhed with demons on the brain
even while life drained from their throats.
At night I kick my wife awake—
never know what I am dreaming.

Louisiana, Late Summer

Because our bodies have been claimed
by humidity, we walk around in our heads
in the heat, squatting in the backroom
to paint a baseboard, sweat
pouring down in fragrant runs,
the ghosts of different body parts
asserting themselves with distinctive odors.

Overhead, a fan twirls lackadaisically,
collecting spoors. Far back in the closet,
a light mold, transported here by some
primeval wind, festers on the toe
of a suede shoe. It pours its cheap
mold life into ignominy and plans
the destruction of the entire world.

Autobiography of a White Girl Raised in the South

"From the day I was born, I began to learn my lessons."
—Lillian Smith from *Killers of the Dream*

In any self-portrait from the '50s, you'd have to see the me
that was not me: the black girl trudging along the side of the road
while I whizzed past in my daddy's car. Or the not-me
girl in the bushes, peeing, while her mama kept watch
and I relieved myself inside, daintily, in the sparkling facilities
of the Southside Esso, labelled WHITES ONLY. All those
water fountains I drank from unthinkingly, the lunch counters
where I disdained my lunch—she was there on the wooden benches
bleached by sun out back of the store, or squatting on a curb
sipping from a Mason jar of tepid water lugged from home,
or eating her sandwiches of homemade biscuits and a smear of fat.

From the beginning, then, there were always two: me and not-me.
The one I was, white and skinny, straight brown hair. And the one
I wasn't, but could've been—that black or brown girl, hair coarser
than mine, eyes darker, skin gleamier and smooth, free of freckles.
I didn't even know where she lived, only saw her in public
when she stepped up on my granny's back porch with a paper bag

of okra, accompanying her mama, selling turnips and tomatoes,
or her daddy, with his tools, come to sharpen the knives.
Then, we eyed each other, I recall, hands behind our backs,
faces solemn and shy, our hair plaited, mine in one long, compliant
tail—but hers in a dozen marvelous sprouts, each tied off
with colored twine. Now, I think it's odd, cruel even,
I never shook her hand, showed off a toy, or asked her out
to my special place in my grandmother's yard,
the powdery patch of gray dust beneath the cherry tree,
where blossoms plopped down in tiny clouds of air and color.
There, cross-legged, knee to knee, we might've touched
each other and satisfied our terrible curiosity—
whether she, in fact, was just like me, and I, like her.
For a moment, sheltered by the blossoms of a flowering tree,
the universe might have seemed to us like the garden
it once was—various and multitudinous, aswarm
with rich textures, interesting odors, a wide palette of color and hue.

Instead, I kept my head down and watched her toes, bare and curled
in the powdery gray-brown dust, and felt envy for her going free
of shoes, and had no idea of the images that might be passing
through her mind. Then I heard my granny's much-loved voice,
calling from the porch, to come away and go inside. She sent away
the not-me's daddy without a sale, and chastised me throughout our lunch
for what she called "familiarity." And through the back screen door,
I saw the not-me girl, walking away behind her daddy, not
looking back, and I heard his voice, querulous, too, chastising
her, as well, for something bad, whatever it was we almost did
but didn't, finally, dare to do.

The Figure Eight

The swan's path is a calm infinity in Boston Common's
public pond. In it, closing back on itself after every turn,
I see the fragile image of my younger brother
in the years before his marriage failed, the rented farmhouse
south of Richmond he shared with friends, laborers
like him at Dupont Chemical. In the evenings,
their gray uniforms dark with sweat, their hair flattened into oily mats,
they squat together on the worn wood steps to smoke
a few joints and guzzle cheap beers, tossing the empties
towards the edge of the wood. They ignore the shattering.
A few minutes of silence before the alcohol kicks in,
its spidery fingers scrambling gratefully in their guts.
And then they're bitching themselves into a state of restlessness—
they've finished with the niggers and the god damned democratic
president, dispensed with the northerners' spiel
on collective bargaining. They're onto women now—
what cunts they are, how all they want is to take you
for a ride. Pissed at the child support somebody's
paying, the abortion another one's wife refused to have.
And without even speaking, they rise and walk down
into the meadow, their cigarettes gleaming weakly in last light,
to the place where the old car rests, a junker someone finagled
for $85 and a lid of hash. An Oldsmobile or something that
glamorous, from the 1950s, once turquoise and sleekly desirable,
Elvis blaring from the perforated speakers in either door,
a shapely car hop leaning down to latch a silver tray of fries
and shakes on the rim of the driver's window. . .
One of them hotwires it alive and my brother slides in, grinning,
lit now, somebody at last, both hands gripping the wheel, and takes off
around the meadow as if—this time—he might really be going somewhere.
His buddies howl when the car stalls out in a deep rut
and then roars to life again, blue smoke breaking
through the back of the engine. The car is whining and popping
with breakage, its back end swinging back and forth, the way
a wounded dog keeps going, homing for its master. The wheels
are straining, like that, trying to move forward,
but he's just going around and around, around
in the mud stiff ruts, somewhere there in the dark cab,
his head cloudy, his mind set on nothing but the figure eight
he's making in the mud, inscribing it deep in the earth
so when God looks down He'll see the sign for infinity,
the same shape of the neat path the swan swims
in the pond at the public gardens where I sit, years away
several lives distant, a universe removed, my hands
shaking, my mouth dry, writing down the words of this poem.

JOHN DOUCET

Le Charivari de Celestin Joseph Doucet

Leeville, 10 August 1867

Through wetting, emerald eyes her mind burns
Flush its porcelain face. I take her head—
Hardened trawl-hands comb her hair's soft turns—
And lay my sacred dreams onto our bed.

I breathe the humid fall of August night
Rising from her skin. My eyes fold closed to still
Her image eclipsing the candle's light.
The silent field beyond the curtained sill

Is stirred by a cackling spirit raised to life:
"*Celestin-Joseph! C'est l'espirit jaleux
De ta Rosalie Cat'rine!*"—my first wife
In the villagers' shrill voices made true.

They drum iron pots and pans and sing my name
Across the marshes. Torches mark their shadows
Through my brightened room. I stand in shame,
A naked figure framed in veiled windows.

A swift August chill protecting her grace,
Retreating beneath her whitening trousseau,
My new bride implores through a cooling face,
"*Va faire du café et des petite gateaux.*"

The Duck Girl of New Orleans

for Giulietta Masina, Fellini's Gelsomina

She was never part of the script, from side streets
as in La Strada, wearing an old hat, evening dress
entirely too long, in high heels that didn't quite fit,
pink ribbons around her wrists and waist, singing
or mumbling to herself, dwarfish and inexplicable,
though not so unlike the young girl in *La Dolce Vita*.

From Pat O'Brian's and *La Casa's*, we toasted her,
we toasted Roland, Eben Flood, Prufrock's burdens,
as if our raison d'êtres were to sing ghostly streets,
menageries of loss in mirrors of *Le Moulin Rouge*,
always slightly inebriated, in the neon wilderness,
whispering lovable lies no less than Fra Lippo Lippi.

The ducks followed her in a marvelous procession,
her quacking choir, entourage of Orleanian indigoes.
Not once did she ever glance aside toward us, our
poetic proposals, serenades in blue, even when we
stopped traffic and followed her down Royal Street,
as now *después tener en cada puerto un amor*.

We come after nuptial plumages, thirty years later
back from the dark abyss, hole that has no bottom,
searching for her, with our fortuitous lives, dressed
in tuxedoes, smoking our cigars, inhaling our rings
of regrets, but *La Casa del Marinero, Gunga Din*
have gone, and Pat O'Brian's fountain is not the same.

We toast the evening at dusk, as the dark comes on,
discuss old men and the sea, the causalities of flesh
near The House of Ursuline, then notice a small figure
from the North, Dauphine Street, white and angelic,
graceful as if she were on ice, gliding with the ease
of Olympian goddesses, with lovely lilacs in her hair.

We are still the princes of allusions, imaginary airs,
but we manage to approach and ask about her ducks.
Her eyes wander off, then back to mine, as if she sees
two of me, as if she almost remembers, or perhaps
to touch Earth one final time. "One day," she says,
her eyes fixed in mine, "they just stopped following."

JAMES ENELOW

On Turning Twenty-six in Lake Charles

Already, all my friends have set their lives,
productively and arrow-aimed at wealth.
With rich and pitying smiles they toast my health
already wondering when I'll have a wife.

Still single at this point, I mar their plans,
they shuffle up their cards and then peruse
the wild card they can't count upon or use;
they'll trade me off and straighten out their hands.

And as the game unfolds they start to fret,
worried I might not even find a date.
They sigh and smile when I approach the gate
alone; they are convinced my life is set.

They grumble and complain and all insist
that I should shuffle into bars and chat,
or take up jogging, get a dog or cat,
to nurture in the need to coexist—

with some nice girl without too many quirks,
alluding to the world I do not share.
But I have played too long at solitaire,
let others count their winning chips and smirk.

And as the year turns slowly in its change,
the last card games line up towards New Year's day,
the last dead leaf outside my house falls away,
the mere mention of plans seems to estrange

those friends from me until they make the break.
I take no invitation as a sign
to tell myself they're only being kind.
I welcome in the New Year with a rake.

I sweep in all the fall's long fallen leaves
and pile them up, each pile a welcome guest
then bag them safely, packed with all the rest
and watch the willows darken near the eaves.

I think about a friend who'd always find
some sugar-coated, cautious thing to say,
but gold outgrows and mulches into gray.
There are some friends we have to leave behind.

Night Writing Without You

for Stephen Gardner

The occasional walnut
drops. And cracks.
And rolls along the tiled roof.

I think of you,
working late, writing,
and think of how the bourbon
mingled with ice,
how your dog's hair
stood on end.

But you aren't here now
to hold back my wailing,
and I feel the poem
inch its way along my spine.
Pictures of poets look down at me;
and the porcelain eyes

of Mexican fertility figures
look down at me,
watch and glaze over.

Somewhere there is a blooding;
somewhere someone's spirit is leaving;
and somewhere a small life starts
the passage of its cycle.
And I am fighting the poem,
fighting to push the words through my fingers
to try and make the white space black.

It comes, winds its way, comes
through the mouths of fertility,
through the eyes of the makers,
rolling, rounding the edges, rushing
to fill the white—and me,
with sleep.

GINA FERRARA

Ginger Lilies

for Maxine Cassin

I want a blade with an agenda
a shiny glint or metallic expanse
sharp, precise and meaningfully serrated
to sever these stalks
momentarily stopped by four nights of frost—
the ones you gave me to plant in the last millennium
a favorite of yours originating
from an Asian jungle where Bengal tigers
and black leopards paced and stalked
amid pendulous shadows
and shrill screeches of Rhesus monkeys.

You promised the lilies would grow into something
beyond fragmentary
spreading like some small town scandal.
Eventually, they took over, dominant
as one side of the brain—
both variegated and solid
topped with dense clusters of blossoms—
their pungent aroma adding spice to the bland wind,
reeds rising to an elevation above flood lines
in this city of our birth.

ANNE MARIE FOWLER

Song of Berries on the Vine

In the darkness, it is hard to make out
the lines of my wanting: the signature
of my heart is spelled out before you.
Can you hear the worms spinning
the ground beneath us? I can't echo
their music; the earth is a magical
harp. No one enters this music hall
but you. You have no reason to trust
the nuance of this tender chord,
but think of harmony, the song
of berries on a vine, how my arms stretch
like ivy around the garden of your body,
the surface of your skin melodious.

JOHN FREEMAN

August Green: A Baptism

A gap in privet led from a mowed field
   to the floor of a leaf pavilion
     so thick that every shade was green:
   the air was stained olive, the shafts of light
     chartreuse. I stood in a dripping heat
where I could not belong, thought it fathered all with root.

I had trespassed on the most ancient of temples, where green
     reaches up to the answering spirit of light.
   I dreamed of sharing with tree and vine
    the mysteries of communion,
to grow from within where the sun's finger touches the leaf.
   But sweat stinging my eyes and skin,

     horsefly, mosquito, and gnat
harried me back through the gap into open field.
   I squinted as wind dried my sweat,
feeling restored in a way I could not name
   but to say the light had watered
     something within me deeply green.

The Yearning, Late October

When dusk has slowly settled like the film
of dust beaten from a rug on the line
and wind shakes old dog-hair leaves from the elms
and growls from the hollow deep in the darkening pines,
a sudden chill rubs up against my spine:
it is time again for my ghosts to come home
to these locked rooms vacated in my mind,
books on the floor, the bed rumpled, just as they left them.

Real as the frost that clouds my window panes,
a mere handful are dead; most still live
on other maps. They drag their ankle chains
and creak along my staircase—fugitives
nourished by our daily bread of pain,
they've journeyed to be forgiven, and forgive.

After Katrina

Returning home, my load of ripped-up carpet
purged into the parish dump, I pass through
these ghost towns one more time—
Bridge City, Westwego, Marrero—
these shells of cracked wood, bent metal,
sheared siding, tarped roofs the foliage
of an artificial blue forest,
the buildings boarded up,
dark, silenced, nobody home.

Day after day like rising water
the mercury has surged over 100.
Exposed metal radiates like a steel foundry,
the sun a crucible of molten iron
pouring its liquid glow down the streets' sluices,
this same heat that boiled up
a hurricane still pounding in our heads
after its rain has flogged these blocks
to a sodden mess like waterlogged rugs.

What if my wife's face were mangled
by car wreck or fire—
sewn skin with brick-red blotches, one eye
a stuck window that can't pry its lid open,
hair falling out like leaves from a dying tree,
a wheelchair from bed to bathroom.
We may never patch over her scars,
and yet she is home, she is home.

Grace

who sits in the booth
at the airport parking lot—
long term—and collects

from me, after my return
through clouds that part
like the gowns of angels

falling, my stamped
ticket and cash,
and who, before I am

released to the highway,
issues me a thin wafer
with her name and a round

smile on it, saying, *Keep this.
This is your receipt. Have
a safe trip home*, has had

so little bearing on
why I left there to begin
with, on the air traffic

control, on the words
I went from here to hear,
that it shocks me to think,

weeks later, of her, her
black-rimmed glasses,
her bleak, Greek face.

What Are Eyes for?

"Shedding" tears, as though
letting them drop meant
putting them in storage.
Whom should I despise

then? What are eyes for, dry,
but to see through whatever
they see and gauge from there
what to assess of what

lies beyond sight. We do,
in other words, cry a lot
for what we have lost
in order to identify

what remains, not what's
immortal, surely—grief
has taught me at least
that much—nor holy,

since it arises from our
crust. Nor lustful, though
the absolute pain seems
to me about the same,

but a thing traced, like
blood, or an awfully
familiar name, unwittingly
unwilling to go away.

I weep to keep that
intact, in fact, don't
you? You think it may
be true? Well, I do, too.

Convalescing

to be restless, but without imagination
to fire your blood jets into steel bars

of presentable art, to sit long, uncomfortable
hours before the mountains of Allah

unmoved, to lose the only dictionary
west of your private Mississippi, to have

an unruly rusty nail driven into your spine
but not to awaken, to whistle a tune

you whistled only yesterday when asked
to respect the bland silence of others, to

lie sleepless, solaced by a slow death
you can depend on, to seem amused

by your president's abuse of office, not
to worry nor wonder where your next meal

has been coming from for some time
now, to believe in the superstitious

but not their superstitions, to be home
without remembering how you arrived,

to be the part of an airmail envelope
neither written on, cancelled, nor licked,

to linger over an unjustified sentence

The Night Café: North Rendon, New Orleans

If we felt generous with ourselves, we drank well,
Basil Hayden's at eight dollars a glass if Les ordered,

Marker's Mark at five-fifty if the tab was mine.
Most of the tables leaned vacantly against their chairs,

The walls exhaling a low shade of green, the kind of room
Van Gogh said a man could lose his mind in.

Our talking threaded through the light and into the dark.
We argued the catalogues of the not-quite-Bob-Dylans—

Then always into further obscurities and personal abstractions,
Tenderness for the women we loved before our wives,

How those romances added up to lives someone chose against;
Entire books we conceived in dreams but did not write, a travelogue

Of the Yucatan Peninsula, a study of empire in Herodotus;
The children we could have had playing in watery shadows

Beneath the billiard tables, watching for a sign of recognition,
Waiting for the names we never gave them to be called.

Whatever failures we recounted would never be trapped
Inside the sweat-rings our cold glasses left on the tabletop,

Their consequences wiped away with the back of a hand.
In the maroon glint of the bathroom's single hanging bulb,

The breasts of vintage centerfolds shone like the night sky
Above Athens just after the Persians torched the city.

We felt our nearest experiences with death and transcendence
Equal to the siege at Thermopylae, captured in our own *Histories*,

Recorded beneath swirls of smoke at a bar on North Rendon,
In the hope of thereby preserving from decay the remembrance

Of what men have done—thus the story opens, told like every tale
That regrets where its ends, murky light rising above the forsaken city.

Faubourg Marigny

I was only drinking Abita on draft
But something buckled me under
Like the century-old smoke of absinthe,
Even before the old Ascension Parish ghost
Picked up his reed and blew.
The wet night air of Frenchmen Street
Set upon me like witches and devils,
Bayou inroads, Crescent City downstep,
Stage lights constellating the ceiling tile.
The trio tested the opening measures
Of "Emancipation Suite,"
                  Free people, free sound,
Each testifying to some greater power
In the open field, the upper registers,
Night sky thundering around us,
Kidd Jordan whistling ribbons of air
Through a tenor saxophone.
                  "Renaissance and Reprise,"
Hamid and William like children born anew
With an upright bass and tabla drum
In place of fingers and hands,
Bright arterial blood coursing the backbeat,
Appendages born to resonate and pulse.
The night ends with a blues, "Decatur Street,"
Sorrowing banished but coming home,
We who witnessed rise from our knees,
Souls doubled in size, spirit grown
Beyond the selves we walked in with,
                  Heading nowhere, together and free.

Bayou Storm in Summer

One entire summer in New Orleans, mornings broke open like fresh eggs,
        cracked and spilled into a blue bowl of sky.

I drank coffee over the kitchen sink, watching sunlight glisten across roof
        shingles as far north as the Fairgrounds.

Some days I smelled the horses making their early sprints. Third floor
        apartment of the tallest house on Crete Street—

I could see the pressbox and the empty top row of bleachers.

By noon the heat was a second suit of clothes, and by three the first drops
        of rain sizzled on the sidewalks.

A storm would erupt, then subside just as quickly, the dead crustacean
        smell swirling, and finally the air cool enough to breathe again.

Then one day I awoke to rattling glass, and the quiet morning had crossed
        over. Clouds rolled in the color of concrete.

The electricity blinked out with the first wave of thunder and I watched as
        lightning skipped across the city.

Water stood and rippled in the street for an hour then streamed off
        underground.

Nothing moved on Esplanade as I crossed toward Bayou St. John—
        Saturday, ten AM and already the air ruptured.

I could smell espresso and fresh bread at CC's Coffee House, where
        I stopped and caught my
breath, but didn't go in, walking instead up DeSoto, past the mute houses.

A man opened a fence and carried some branches to the curb. He
shrugged and smiled.

The Bayou never gleamed beautifully as it curled through Mid-City, but this
        morning the bowels
of every Mississippi River tributary south of Minnesota seemed flushed
        into New Orleans.

Hurricane Katrina was two years away, but I could see the future in miniature spinning upstream in the murk—

Dry socket of a war just begun, blood and oil swirling together, everyone
feeling wire-tapped, no child left behind, and across town the lower Ninth
Ward strapped to the mast of a ship not yet sinking—

A mud-slaked turtle swiveled past in the current, dragged into the light, as
      though the whole
      floor of the river had been swept up,
            with no place to settle but the back of my throat.

CHRIS HANNAN

Acquamorta

Acqua chiusa, sonno delle paludi
che in larghe lamine maceri veleni,
ora bianca ora verde nei baleni,
sei simile al mio cuore.
            —Salvatore Quasimodo, *Acquamorta*

The batture clings
around the knees
and gnarled limbs

of bald cypresses
and snagged driftwood
like old cartilage.

This soil lies
eroding as winter
currents stretch past

ligaments of levees.
Silt banks, sagging
as thighs, straddle

the fall's alluvion:
not quite earth
nor river's surge

but mud hovering
between the waters.
Eddies like gasps

reveal something unmoved
where the depths,
blood-thick with loam,

scour these shoals,
scleroses of tides
and riparian clay,

where you sink
ankle-deep and smell
the dusk quickening.

RABIUL HASAN

Blue Birds

Blue birds live among ten blue faces.
I am one blue face blue birds love to soothe,
but I return to you at the end of the day
the way a sojourner returns home when he is gray.

I could love you better, but I am poor as the lonely man
speaking only to himself as he retreats to his shell at nightfall.
I am small now, crestfallen, ignominious in my defeat, for claiming you.
Sunlight darkens in the breasts of blue birds streaking past the nova.

I become airborne like them and do not alter course.
I am humble as a stubble of grass beside the roughage.
What use do I have for Mona Lisa and Geronimo now?
I strain and expiate; you will absolve me when you have loved me.

ASHLEY MACE HAVIRD

Dirt Eaters

Their time near, Delta women with no use
for doctors know to gather dauber nests
for a silty tea to ease their child
into this world. To heal the navel,
a poultice, rust-brown, like raw clay,
that dries brittle—
a shard some keep and treasure.

Summer's end, my daughter leaves home.
As in the weeks before her birth, I clean
everything in sight—even the porch screens
of our century-old house. Unhinged,
hauled outdoors for their first scrub-down
in years, they reveal, clotting the channels
that anchor our floor-to-ceiling louvers,
clumped fingers of mud dauber nests.
I hack at them with a screwdriver.

I never saw the wasps at work,
welding their nests into these grooves,
toting stunned spiders
to cradleboards where larvae hatched and fed.
On hands and knees, I sweep
catacombs crumbling with leggy remains—
wasp or prey?
The nest-dust salts my eyes,
grits my tongue.

Sideshow

What stopped us en route
to Moesgaard Museum's
Amazing Bog Man
was unspectacular—an unearthed grave:
the skeleton of a dog
whose human had taken pains
to fix its limbs as if it slept mid-chase.
The bones were Stone Age bones
from a dolmen that crouched in sea-fog
overlooking Aarhus Bay.
A good dog—surely guard or guide—
to be honored by ceremony.

Grauballe Man was a length of twisted jerky
that took our appetite.
A shock, the tannin-hennaed hair,
clown-grimace, throat-gash,
blood poured into the gullet
of some thirsty god
biding its time in that soggy underworld . . .

"I miss Hector," our daughter said
of our Lab, back in the States.

                        *   *   *

After ten years I'd forgotten
that skeleton already ancient
when Iron Age Grauballe began his curing—
until, still unbalanced from the fall
of New York's towers, I watched on TV
teams searching for anything human.
I focused on the dogs
stumbling atop the debris,
mouthing what we have no stomach for.

On our walks—Hector's and mine—
now gunmetal evenings
smother too early the sun,
I recall survivors' accounts of tidal waves—

of looking up bewildered, mistaking
for a dark arcing cloud
the scythe that was the sea.
I sometimes stop on these walks,
bend my head to his
and whisper for no good reason
"Good dog." And his breath
is a warm and fishy fog.

Nights, he lays his head
like a twitching brick on our feet,
staying us.

Resurrection: Ivorybill

Men drowning dream of flight.
Their bones thin into stems of cattails,
their arms leaf out. Beneath the swamp
water's skin of sky, believing
in the rising of their changed bodies,
they mistake for storm-stripped crowns
the labyrinth of roots. At rest
within the bottomland forests they felled,
they grieve us back into the world.

From the stumps of the Tensas, an uprush—
a dream? Beneath the oar
beat of my wings,
a child, sprawled on a mud flat,
its eyes reflecting my yellow eyes . . .
a dog, its leathered carcass hung
by floodwaters in a scrub oak. North,
towards the smell of swamp decay
and the sharp sweet lily, the rumor of a mate,

I turn the sky aside,
row to this diminished wood.
No red wolf's song, no panther's rip.
Only the rumor—they speak it, the living men
who disguise themselves as trees
and whisper in tree-tongue.
Like the cypresses, they stalk the river.
From them, I have learned to be sly.
Quieter now, I tear into rot-soft Tupelo
and rake the crawling meat.

My shadow falls over water ash
and buttonbush, swamp rose
and lizard's tail, heron and hawk,
the banded water snake,
swarms of frogs small as horseflies,
and men dreaming that I am God.
The rumor of a mate carries me.
The blades of my wings
feather the sky, fan out the sun.

DAVID HAVIRD

A Wind of Goats

Flat Rock / Asheville / Arden, North Carolina

At Connemara a trail
led from the house to the barn
(Carl Sandburg's wife had bred
goats that won blue ribbons),
tripped alongside hedges
and where it outpaced them: wind.
A champion herd, ice-horned.

The front had begun as a blustery horde
of country cousins at Biltmore House. The tour
at an end, "I like this part"—
servants' quarters, kitchen and laundry,
the basement—"best,"
one elderly woman drawled to another. "You would,"
I thought. Though truth be told,
me too. *The people, yes,*
the people. A Greyhound full.
Reagan / President / Reagan,
their campaign buttons read, and *give 'em Helms*—
Jesse, that is, the state's race-baiting senator
up for reelection. Jostled,

I saw myself, a boy, beside the carport,
three neighborhood kids accosting me
there on the flagstone walkway beside the white
camellias. "Nigger-lover," one of them sneered,
the flat of his hand slamming the wind from my chest.
It got out *how*—we were for LBJ.

Night finds us knotted together, the thermostat not
to be found, my wife and me and my father.
When autumn reddened the Blue Ridge,
this drive was an annual thing
for him and my mother. We've missed the color, he grouses.
The friends of my parents whose holiday cabin this is—
they lent me when I was a kid
LPs of Sandburg reading. Picture

the boy on his back, lights off in the foyer,
in front of the Magnavox. Here
on the cover of *Honey and Salt*,
the white-maned poet has bundled himself in a scarf.
The dry leaves trampled, the herd,
butting the tree trunks, crashes with one held bleat
through the branches—where
among the goats are the sheep? And if, through the fog
of our exhalations, a flurry of cold
reaches my face, I hold my breath—
a dream-disheveled child
afraid that if he lets it out,
his mother's fingers, fussing now with his hair,
will whisk it away.

Smoking in Bed

For Elizabeth Spencer

"Whenever I pass a field of artichokes,
I picture Venus beneath it." For me it's fields
of tobacco and Marilyn Monroe,
her nude body discovered. . . Nude?
Naked, my parents explained. In bed
naked? I was bewildered. My dad at the wheel
of our two-tone green '58 Impala,
my parents and I on our way to Ocean Drive
where Grandmother Rainwater kept a house. . . Nearby,
a beach-front novelty store. I bought a toy cigar,
teased out wads of confetti, and stuffed it with leaves
filched from a warehouse en route. (Tobacco auctions
were something to see.) The tip alight with red glitter,
I'd smoke that enormous cigar and savor the secret.
Summers running together, I married a woman
whose family farmed tobacco. . . who breathed the fields
distilled, the sweated heat of oven-tight barns,
with Mr. Phil inspecting the wooden barns
where leaves, tied up in hands and hanging from sticks,
turned yellow. In Martha Ingram's account
a peasant unearths with his plow a Venus with arms
and legs and a head "mindless" and "lovely." Posed
on a shelf at the novelty store, inflatable dolls
with corn-silk hair. The bathing suit was red.
Squeeze the tummy and naked breasts pop out.
Plastic telescopes, cherry and lemon and grape,
Popsicle colors—with these I spied on women
captured without any clothes. The idol intact.
I picture my raven-haired mother in deeper
than ever, her latex bathing cap a skull.
She brought it up with her feet, a rose-lipped shell
that came to rest—the conch so stank up the car—
in spikes of weed along the highway home.
Martha's Italian farmer replanted his Venus.
If word got out, they'd designate his fields
a "site." Barely awake, rousted from bed
at 5 for the drive to the beach, I follow
a dark-haired girl—in 1962
we both turn 9—down rows of tobacco—
the top leaves only remain on the plants—
traipsing beside her grandpa. They halt at the pack house.
The leaves are loose now and lying in heaps on burlap.
The ravishing smell of cured tobacco,
the ghost of green fields, gilds the August heat.

How One Became Two

When Gretel was small, she told
the secret no one must ever tell.
The ironing board stood between

her and her mother, the woman ironing.
What Gretel remembers is this: the iron
sliding across the backs of her hands

and the freezing cold
that came at first and spread
up her arms to her chest

and how she stood back from the board
awed, the odd meat smell,
the woman's long hair striking

the air like cottonmouths,
the single whir of the clock
and the way it did not proceed.

How Gretel herself seemed to grow
a little taller, sandals and sunsuit gone
and her clothes become a white wool robe

and how her hair went white blond
and floated straight and fine
on air currents the skin could not feel,

mouth falling open slow motion
in nothing more than surprise,
eyes fixed flat as an icon's.

The iron made a clucking sound
and her hands—while she was staring
at them, cold as snow—

ignited. Flamed up yellow-red
like fire forced before bellows—and
it was all she could see,

those burning hands. What might
they do? What could she touch
they would not destroy?

The clock lurched forward at last,
and she fell back and ran to the mirror.
She thought she'd see the child

in white wool with burning hands,
but instead of one she saw two—
twins, a boy and a girl.

The girl, with only a small diminishment
in weight, looked down at her hands,
opening and closing. She could see

every line, knuckle, scar, unmistakable
as initials. The boy felt quite hollow
and set about learning to do

all over again. He found
he was very clever
and always afraid.

That was a different mother.
That was before the story began.

All the Men in My Family Hunt

I don't hear the alarm. Usually
I don't even wake up when you leave.
You drive up together to George's land
in the Felicianas, to hunt wild turkey.
Thermos, coffee breath, jokes in the truck.
Jokes women wouldn't laugh at, jokes
about too much bourbon, the girl
who couldn't get enough. I move over
into the warm spot on your side.

George told me you have to be in the woods
a full hour before first light, someplace
you've seen the birds before, and there
you make the sound of an owl.
Turkeys hate owls so much, they stir
on their roosts and grumble in their sleep.
My mother once told me Daddy heard an owl
the night before he died. I asked her later
what kind of owl it is you hear before you die.
She said, the owl who knows your name.

Anyway, George says you listen for that hoarse gobble
and haul ass toward it, shotgun vertical
in front of you so the stickers won't cut your face.
You can't see. You try to get yourself
into range the exact moment of gray dawn.
If you're early, you'll run up too close, and
they'll hear you before you can see to take aim.
If you're late, they see you coming and fly off
before you're close enough to shoot.

The window by the bed begins to show its frame.
I remember daylight, maybe afternoon.

I'm nine or ten, I walk behind his slumping bulk
for miles, carrying the shotgun. Bisque colored road ruts
fill with sweet gum leaves, with sycamore sticks,
the cold gun barrel bumps its bruise of honor
against my skinny collarbone. At some signal
I do not hear, he lightens, turns like a dancer
and takes the gun, whispers, *Be quiet.*
Later—I'd stood at attention for half an hour—

he comes back uphill, shakes his head, which is all
the story I expect, and there the memory leaves off.

I know what wild turkey looks like
only from the whiskey bottle, but I ate it once
at your mother's—firm, deep-brown meat,
even the breast. It was Thanksgiving,
we were grateful. A dense earth taste
like gun smoke, black walnuts, tar.
In the pillows and the empty bed,
I'm rousing with the urge to kill and eat.
I was 22 years old and we'd just got married.
All the men in my family hunt. Jokes
women wouldn't laugh at *anymore*, I mean:
back then I used to laugh at them during dinner.
Under the covers, I move my legs to find the place
you left, and half-dream you and George

waiting under sable trees, when you can't see
each other's features or even uprightness,
imitating animal calls you practiced driving up.
Listening for the grumpy sounds of sleep,
running full tilt in the slap dark, guns loaded,
falling across stream beds, armadillo holes, crashing
through blackberries and sticker vines you'd duck under
any other time. Chasing—we are all chasing,
the dream is ending—chasing the shy wild bird I tasted
only that once, I still remember it in my mouth.
Trying to be the owl who knows its name.

On the Question of Angels

Thump. Bird-crash
into the window. I wince
and—brief sin—hope
it's the mockingbird

that woke us up so early,
expounding secondhand repertoire.
Rising sun shoots straight at me,
backlights the splat of goo

and feathers stuck on the pane.
In warming air, soft currents
stir the thumb-sized mess and,
can you believe it, there's an angel

hovering with spread wings.
Splintered feathers swing
like arms raising a chorale score
for an alto to sight-read

White and gray choir robe—it WAS
the mockingbird—ruffles in slow flight.
Call it suicide mission:
credo / collision / death / angel.

Call it the misery of the world,
the grisly accidents, murderous
barriers, random enemies,
aimless war on whatever

wants nothing more than to sing.
Call it the demise of a bird
that may be the very one come
to tell us what we all long to know.

DIXON HEARNE

Native Cure

She bends and rubs the black salve on her swollen leg,
Hikes her skirt into a knot mid-thigh.
Cypress knees rise through the ground fog
Like spirits climbing from the fetid swamp,
The airs grow heavy with resin and decay,
Pains pitch and roll from knee to toe's end.

Crouching low, she shapes a pile of potions,
Rubbing them between her hands,
Chanting in an ancient tongue.
Lighting the fire, widening her eyes
As smoke charms writhe, swirl to meet her—
A dark and healing ritual,
But she must hurry,
While daylight still holds potency
To work its magic.

Shadows quicken
To chase the venom
From her veins
And send it back
Into the moccasin's mouth.

JACK HEFLIN

Local Hope

From tangle of water oak, from willows torn free upriver
as far as Felsenthal,
         from bank waste freed from bean field levees,
  from cotton rot, from egrets sipping soggy bottoms, hunting perch,
from cottonmouths tossed like scarves along
    the elegant arms of driftwash,
        from all of this and from the maternal hush of water
distilled before thunder comes the clumsy swish and thump of
    Walmart flipper, extra-large, comes the mumbled
curses, comes the aftershock sighting . . .
                           what's left of him:
thin-shinned splash of a lost olympian gone dunking for God.
       He tugs his goggles, no looking back, floating past
  where he began, kicking a wake of
         arrogance and rage, suspiciously thirsty,
    a blackout draft he'll take all night to drink, cracker thick,
  full of fertilizer and factory scabs, full of mongoloids,
magnolia blooms,
         rafts his fathers built of tar and poker chips,
shattered pitching wedges, sand-bag second mortgages,
    sepia letters, portraits from which no one ever smiles:

All the good men who learned too late they'd never love.

  He chokes it down and bottoms up.
                  He forgets his dream,
but in the fiction-blood of current
      he dreams, he paddles and scrawls,
                 he lunges to the Baptist deeps,
    past the piscicultural and the multi-piscicultural,
past whole families fishing for Jesus,
              past runaways
     picking the bones of a carnival,
  past loggerhead and eel, past moonshine,
roadstand pickled fishfin, past grennel and gar,
             backstroking, back,
    all the way back,
    birthing himself with each breath

until said host of swollen atavism comes dripping out,
pulling its tail,
slug mud lost beyond the shoreline wrecks rusting phosphorescent
in this paramouric slip of river
bruised by flood, bream bed,
rip-rap glistening in the mythical dawn.
Water picks the chassis clean.

Farther down from lock and dam, there are only parts,
rear ends and shocks, children dozing over buckets of catfish,
all you can eat. The locals laugh
but like to rub their little heads for luck.

The CAT-Scan

I slip into the lead jacket, tighten the lead collar,
and at last my worry wears its own weight,
has become something more than abstraction
or superstition as it did yesterday when I went
running and told myself if I could make five miles
the X-ray would find nothing, that his little head
would look as normal inside as it looks outside,
red hair and rusty freckles, dimpled, doughy cheeks.
Now he's fitted on the sled and will soon pass
through what looks like, he tells me, a doughnut,
his head a loaf of bread wedged in its tray.
He believes somehow it will make the pain
go away, and how can I explain otherwise,
even mention the word tumor, a word
so thick it loads the air above our heads
if we work the courage up to call its name.
I answer his question *why* a hundred times a day,
why for instance do we have to eat and why
in sleep we dream some things we'll never do.
I no longer count my white inventions lies.
He's holding still, trying even not to blink.
How much he respects us all, our instructions,
technologies, my half-cooked approximations
about how this world works. How fast it leaves
us all behind with few ideas to offer in return.
He's given his blood without a wince and
now the technicians withdraw, the terrible
whirring begins, the ticks and clicks which trace
this other truth about our lives. He slides forward,
red lasers mark his face, and I'm holding fast,
my hand locked around his ankle, my fingers crossed.

The Bad Caddie

You were born to waste your life.
                    —Louis Simpson

For James Crumley

        Maybe you should go for a walk,
take your shoes from the dog's mouth,
                        leave a tip, get powdered,
spend the day looking for lost balls
        in the high rough
                        running down Country Club Road,
numbers three, thirteen—cave hole!—
        the dogleg (no relation) ninth.

    Then the long climb to the unclaimed lots,
                    out there along the edge of what
the more experimental republicans
                        call wilderness
        (the ditches I mean) and where by contrast

you feel best, sunk as you are up to your nuts
        and beating with a titanium wand

this godsown welter of matter & facts: the nature and
            waste, effluvium et cetera,
        one finds at the borders of a board game
            writ such as this:
                        wilted azaleas,
cocktail plastic, the mower's shed,
        the hand opening to receive its tip,
                            chemical trauma,
        the boneyard of old pros,
                red by-god American ants:
        the basic elements of the universe
    (in translation):
                    Bic lighters, abandoned carboys,
    the flatulent half-life of the disposed.

        What memories! Balata rubber, ink, all
    but a few bites of a radar burrito, a wrinkled napkin
kissed with a belch: The pick of the litter, my man,
                    for sale as far as you can see,
        a fairway near the dump, a future.
                        Think about it,

somewhere to love:
              its corners claimed, the half-pint somersaults
        in a flattened parabola
              above the Riviera's busted taillight,
    a last-prayer hook shot missing wide,
        exploding in a wreck of whiskey light
    against an empty quart of Busch:

    and in that spark is born your love,
              distilled, full-lipped, wanting more.

Call it luck,
        you call it a wand,
     it looks more like the left-handed
wedge from your father's bag
        rotting slowly there in the basement,
              a bag of shag balls
idling in the ooze. From a distance (and I can't tell you
    how important perspective is here)
because you're short and thin,
                  you look
a little weedy, unsheltered,
     a long walk from a rain shack
        (if you know what I mean)
should it come a sudden hail of birdie dust.

     It's a contact sport, occasionally toxic.
              (Upon hearing the shouted "fore,"
the player should cup his hands behind his head,
     covering the ears, eyes the temples,
and never look up.)

     Keep your head down, wear a cap.
                  You're a man of impossible lies,
and by all estimations and actuaries,
          just another goofy bastard beside the road,
  suffering in the trash for us all,
              stepping from behind a tree, zipping up,
     spilling the rocks from his shoes,
his sack full, a Dump Family Singer wandering
his way out of it all, whatever it was
     he wanted to say: *I once ate a shoe.*
                  See:
     there's nothing to say. No movie, no movie credits,

     but quite a racket
released from the last row of Mercer's Theater, 1965,

golf balls, by the buckets, all galloping
toward the screen at just the perfect moment
        in *Gone With the Wind*,
                        Rhet Butler whipping

        a blinded mare for the collapse of a culture
burning there on the scaffold of Selznicks's
        Hollywood set.
                        It was your best joke,

but who will defend these Titleists, Maxflis,
        men of real distinction?
                        With your wand you beat them all,
            anoint their ecstatic relocation,
                Saint Catabolism,
the two-toned party balls (considered omens),
        the Slazengers James Bond sliced to the heath,
            a single Pink Lady
                        who weeps in your pocket.

        Before you know it, the afternoon assumes
its shape, out and back,
                        a bit warped from round,
scuffed, smudged.
                    Liking the ruse, you lingered
        like a salesman warmed by the sun,
            offered for inspection your dimpled gems,
    your lost anarchy, tattooed, minimally logoed,
                                inappropriate,

        but loud enough to wake a ghost
(pick a president)
                    dozing there near the tee box,
        puzzled with the slow play, now awake,
                caught between clubs
                                (must he choose wrong?)
        a bit too happy with himself,
perfect statue of it all. He never knew what to say.

        The cave hole, remember? A hard right
through the pines, the hole that always
                    gave him trouble—two nine irons,
        maybe eights, an eight or a nine?

        What will you tell him?
You're the bad caddie.
                    You're damned if you know.

CAROLYN HEMBREE

Rigging a Chevy into a Time Machine
& Other Ways to Escape a Plague

1.   Rig your Chevy into a time machine:
             copper lips copperhead tattoo stag
             stiletto. Eyecandy thrusts her hips
             thumbs through belt loops—1-2-1-2
             2 bottles of Boone's, 1 Chevy bed
             unzip studded jeans along the inseam
             her tan line—your Indian summer

2.   Kill the harbinger at your screen door:
             call the opossum (milk carton in hand)
             like a cat, "here thing"
             loose a flo
             the trick's to aim high
             to make that marsup fly

3.   Ironclad your nerves:
             should a spirit hassle the hackberry
             cast it out. 20 paces or so to the cement ledge
             the crumbling step that's overgrown
             each yellow vine that hooks your heel
             face the grove
             it runs acres, acres north
             clang a cast-iron skillet with a serving fork
             then when a mile round
             tines vibrate (the fork's and the stag's)
             for the hills the stag will run. that's the spirit
             hold still. the place where a fawn's nestled

4.   Have a boy:
             tinsel scotched to the screen door

5.   Have a girl:
             Adeline

6.   Sort the cold from the feverish:
             wanderlust from wandering lost
             succor from suture

the cold the feverish
burn their bedclothes

7.   Work the signs:
        in the burnt-out filling station
        in milk crates copperheads
        a glass harmonica
        players wet fingers
        a blue jay nest
        a kid with the fever taps a freckled shell
        baby, baby, did you caw? did you caw?
        Eyecandy in tongues, her apple
        cheeks, her upper lip stuck to her teeth
        Eyecandy's fingernails glitter and fleck off

8.   Abbreviate:
        sooner or later we all got to molt

9.   Drive, fly you lucky bastard—
        from rose fever from milk poison
        from crumps from landfills drive
        before your luck is up
        before you spy yourself in the buffed chrome
        of a Chevy truck up on concrete blocks

10.   Try an opossum sequel:
        simple—buy a gun

11.   Let bygones:

12.   Peak into outer space:
        an eyeball through the treillage
        your fingers through the treillage
        through wormhole after wormhole

13.   Take the host:
        your incisors tweeze stamen from honeysuckle

14.   Face the ghosts:
        those twin petal lobes you've unbuckled

JESSICA HENRICKSEN

Blaze

Not yet midsummer,
the mimosas hang their fronds
like splayed meats inside the sun's white maw.
Severe, this heat advisory for Louisiana,
lawns seconds from snapping into smoke,
and sprawled the dogs, all tongue,
in the one shady nook, a ditch
dug out beneath burnt yellow
gardenia bushes.

It's June,
my birth month, a moth
stitched to a rotted book's binding,
and again I'm trying for the song
worth exhuming.

If it's Recollection, recall
my mother's collection of remnants:
porcelain knobs spun from cupboards, fallen
finials, swatches of silk for the Austrian plume
curtains she would sew for the living room.
Each relic a gong across the heart's still pond,
and hung from her life's hinge, I would have married
her armoire, grown old a curator
of orphaned Staffordshire.

If it's Marriage, recall
my mother's hands like misplaced moons
mounting the beast's disloyal mirror; the years with him
burnished her into smoke. She was never meant
to look like that, a ghost stoking the air
for another's stars to roost.

If it's Childhood, recall
my mother's brush sweeping my scalp,
one hundred strokes tugging the tangles.
Memory dials up a steep stairwell of detritus, my room
at the end of a cool wooden rail, a clavicle of shadow

spiraling fragments of sword—not that that house
was ever my protector. No window nursed
my wrists to take a quickened pulse.

If it's Retelling The Story, recall
her madness. A scattering of gulls, gape rent
in the night-gallery into which more gaping flows. Mother
to child, child to mother, mother to him, her husband—
how his thunder ossified to stone. In her story,
chapters trapeze a whorl of broken lyres, blare
a sickle-narrative of disinheritance
she still carries,
flares.

Tell me, what shower
can unburden this blaze? I soak rags in a basin,
pat down the dogs; each doused swatch forces more fever
from this month's furnace, wrings out the web-width
of my birth's handbarrow that would shuttle
this long summer, infernal arc of song,
toward more shadow.

Soaked

How do we measure wetness, gauge intensity
of drenchedness? Is it in the round yeasty
odor left after any August afternoon's
unexpected rainfall, or in the stench of piss
on the alley's wall behind the Come And Get It
Lounge? Let us take a moment to applaud
wetness—all the gutters gushing into rivers
roiling into basins of lakes winding wild waste
to even wetter oceans. Sluice gate to trough
deep and slopping. Storms of marvel, do I
name what seeps my heart through, loamy
childhood of mud pies, mid-life's homelessness
and hoping? Shake me up a cocktail, Hurricane,
of more rot and blossom, spin me out
for miles without direction. I'll walk your
oily streets, my sandals soaked in triumph.

Subsidence I

A shock of flood. My father waits in the living room.
His house is gently shaking in the dark room pan. The pilings
are pins. My father waits every day for the newspaper, the mailbox not truly
floating, its red flag a sail. My father waits in the living room. The radio
    with last week's
battery. The cat jumps from the wide camper's room to the tree, then deck.
The motors are killed.
The motors are killed.
My father waits in the living room.

Rainbow Trout

The first fish we knew. *Look for color,*
said Uncle James, *like oil puddled.*
He swore, carved model boats,

had gray-green tattoos, naked she-devils
straddling a submarine. *It used to be*
red and blue, he said.

We cut poles of bamboo, hiked
Sonoma Creek, fishing light with our eyes.
Walk softly, he said, *every step*

sends circular waves they can feel.
I stamped, my job to disbelieve.
A trout leapt, sun silvering its back.

Not one bite shivered our hand-
wound lines that day. Punishment
for doubt and clumsy feet,

but on my hook, too weak to pull,
dangled a thumb-sized fry,
and because it died, I carried it home,

cupped like a pet in my palm.
My uncle cooked it crisp in butter,
so small I ate the bones.

Don't save the damn head,
my uncle said, but I slipped
the dime-sized skull

into my napkin, amazed
at the size of my hands.
Outside I played at war,

salted flesh still on my lips,
each step quick as a prism fish,
sonar waves scattering.

JULIE KANE

Ode to the Big Muddy

1.

Because I grew up a half-hour's drive
from the North Atlantic, always within reach
of the dried-blood-colored cranberry bogs,
the ice bucket water, the desolate beach
with its circular rhythms, I looked down
on linear things, so like an erection
straining against a blue-jeans zipper,
always pushing in the same direction,
spine for brains. But I have learned to mimic,
quick for a girl, the river's predilection.

2.

The first time I saw the Mississippi,
under the curving wing of a jet plane,
it lay there listless as a garden slug:
glistening, oozing, brown. Surely Mark Twain's
paddlewheel visions, Hart Crane's hosannas
to the Gulf, Muddy Waters's delta blues
hadn't sprung forth from a drainage canal?
"Fasten your seatbelts for descent into
New Orleans. Looking to the left, you'll see
the Mississippi River"—so it was true.

3.

Unlike the ocean, the river's life is
right on the surface, bobbing there like turds:
a load of tourists on the *Delta Queen*
drunkenly singing half-remembered words
to show tunes played on steam calliope;
the push boats nudging at oil tankers;
and nothing underneath but chicken necks
in crawfish nets, and our own dropped anchors.
The sea is our collective unconscious;
the river our blank slate, growing blanker.

4.

And yet the river gathers memories:
the ugliest things grow numinous
over time—the trail of a garden slug
crystalline, opaline, luminous
when the garden slug itself has gone
as the river itself will one day go,
already trying to change its course—
an afternoon we watched the ferryboat
go back and forth until the sun went down,
skimming the water like a skipping stone.

5.

Or the morning we gave back Everette's ashes:
homeless alcoholic poet-prince.
A cold March wind was ruffling the water.
Wouldn't you know, the ashes wouldn't sink,
so someone jumped in to wrestle them under.
It hit me then: I didn't want to die.
And so I made a choice, against my nature,
to throw my lot in with that moving line:
abstract, rational, conscious, sober,
cutting a path through human time.

Egrets

You have to love them
for the way they make takeoff
look improbable:

jogging a few steps,
then heaving themselves like sacks
of nickels into

the air. Make them wear
mikes and they'd be grunting
like McEnroe lobbing

a Wimbledon serve.
Then there's the matter of their
feet, which don't retract

like landing gear nor
tuck up neatly as drumsticks
on a dinner bird,

but instead hang down
like a deb's size tens from
the hem of her gown.

Once launched, they don't so
much actively *fly as blow*
like paper napkins,

so that, seeing white
flare in a roadside ditch, you
think, *Trash or egret?*—

and chances are it's
not the great or snowy type,
nearly wiped out by

hat plume hunters in
the nineteenth century, but
a common cattle

egret, down from its
usual perch on a cow's
rump, where it stabs bugs.

Whoever named them
got it right, coming just one
r short of *regret*.

RICHARD KATROVAS

Blues' Body

The souls of drunks bob in the rafters
and a keen, gray glow shimmers the counter.

Fish-faced old man stirs me a cool one
out of what is left of night.

He spins the rocks glass into the air
to glaze it with Pernod, then pours my seventh Sazarac.

Only now, in this light, at this time,
in these states of Louisiana and Inertia

will Blues' body show itself:
Creole hermaphrodite decked in denim and chiffon.

From the electric-blue dawn she enters,
trolling her wrap over the parquetry.

The bartender rolls his somnolent eyes,
sees, blinks slowly, and turns to the well.

Layering six liqueurs
over a spoon-lip into a double-shot jigger

he says nothing. She turns the *Pousse l'amour*
in the lamplight and is satisfied

then closes her eyes and sips, pinky erect,
the Secret of Life etched on her broad bicep:
Mama love Daddy
but he be dead

Love Poem for an Enemy

I, as sinned against as sinning,
Take small pleasure from the winning
Of our decades-long guerrilla war.
For from my job I've wanted more
Than victory over one who'd tried
To punish me before he died,
And now, neither of us dead,
We haunt these halls in constant dread
Of drifting past the other's life
While long-term memory is rife
With slights that sting like paper cuts.
We've occupied our separate ruts
Yet simmered in a single rage.
We've grown absurd in middle age
Together, and should seek wisdom now
Together, by finishing this row.
I therefore decommission you
As constant flagship of my rue.
Below the threshold of my hate
You now my good regard may rate.
For I have let my anger pass.
But, while you're down there, kiss my ass.

DAVID KIRBY

Psychodynamic Electrohelmet

Fellows, it's happened to us all: you're having
    a glass of wine with a beautiful woman at an outdoor
        café, and the weather's nice, sunny and cool but not too,
and she's wearing this floral-print dress, and one
        of the straps keeps sliding down her arm, and she keeps
    putting it back on her shoulder but finally
decides just to let it lie there, and you're feeling pretty sexy, pretty

happy about the way things are going and confident
    that they're going to get better, when suddenly her eyes
        roll up in her head and she says, "Some people are
doorways to other worlds." What are you going to do at times
        like this other than give credit
    to whoever came up with the phrase, "What are you
going to do?" Why, just the other day, I was putting out the trash,

and my neighbor Richard walks by with his wife Kim,
    and as I'm lowering the bag into the bin, Richard looks
        up and says, "Nice trash," and I'm thinking, Richard
doesn't know a thing about my trash, and then I realize
        he's just making small talk, is trying to be nice himself.
    I say there's a lot to be said for niceness,
especially in light of all the stupidity out there: this morning

in the paper, it said that masterpieces are always being
    stolen not because there's a Dr. No paying top dollar
        for Manets and Picassos to hide away on his secret island
but because art thieves think there's a Dr. No paying
        top euro for Van Goghs and Gauguins to hide away
    in his secret castle. The art thieves have
forgotten their Plato, who says, in the Phaedrus, that we must

carve nature at its joints, that is, that the world is made
    of parts that divide cleanly when we're thinking right,
        though when we're not, we're like drunk butchers swinging
blindly at a carcass, our dull choppers bouncing off sinew
        and bone. But you can't stop people from having ideas,
    especially wrong ones. Where do we go when we leave
this earth? On the shore of tiny Aldeburgh, on the coast

of Suffolk, I saw a war memorial that said, "They who
   this monument commemorate were numbered among
     those who, at the call of king and country, left all
that was dear to them, endured hardship, faced danger,
     and finally passed out of the sight of men."
   Where's that, though? In a dream once, I was wearing
my psychodynamic electrohelmet, which is like a fifties football helmet

with a single-bar face mask and an electric cord with a plug
   you stick into a wall socket. My psychodynamic electrohelmet
     would have explained everything to me, but I never got
to use it. I was at my parents' house even though I was
     the age I am now, whereas they were younger than me even
   though they're my parents and have themselves passed
from the sight of men. And then I was in France.

And then the dream was out west somewhere, though
   this time I wasn't in it any more, just a lot of cowboys,
     and some had clown noses while others wore tutus.
My psychodynamic electrohelmet would be a miracle
     of rare device, and with it I would build a pleasure dome,
   sunny but with caves of ice, and a beautiful woman
there, and honeydew, and I'd drink the cherry cola of Paradise.

On Learning That I Share a Birthday
with Jean-Martin Charcot (1825-1893)

It includes writers who bore me to sobs, the list of those
who share my birthday: not only Louisa May Alcott
        but her father Bronson, of whom Robert D. Richardson, Jr.,
author of *Emerson: The Mind on Fire*, wrote
"Alcott had a thin streak of genius, but . . . little talent for writing,"

        though there are also such excellent actors as Don Cheadle
and Cathy Moriarty as well as ones you never hear much
        about any more like Andrew McCarthy and such comics
    as Garry Shandling and Howie Mandel and musicians
like Chuck Mangione and John Mayall as well as the Billy Strayhorn

        who wrote both "Lush Life"and "Take the A Train" and, best
of all, Donizetti! Domenico Gaetano Maria Donizetti,
        whose name alone makes you happy even if the screamingly
    funny *La Fille du Régiment* doesn't, which it does! Then there's
the good writers, including Willie Morris, Carlo Levi,

        and Madeleine L'Engle, whose juvenile sci-fi I prefer to
the freight-laden words of C. S. Lewis, also born on the 29th,
        not to mention the hair-splitting ones of Georges Poulet,
    also born that day and one of the greatest names
in literary theory—in every sense! Then there are the statesmen,

        always suspect, alas, the states being the nests of vipers they are,
and these include such different types as Jacques Chirac,
        President of the French Republic, and the Rev. Adam
    Clayton Powell, Jr., of Harlem, member of the U.S.
House of Representatives and serial misappropriator of funds that

        allowed him to display rather more wealth than someone
should who represented a poor district. But talk about
        names that make people happy—Busby Berkeley!
    All you have to say is "Busby Berkeley," and even a Martian
would get a picture of bosomy blondes scissoring their legs in

        complex geometric patterns! But nobody gets happy when
you say Jean-Martin Charcot, who was kind of an idiot. . . .
        The main thing he did was give Freud a shot in the arm,
    but before that, Charcot documented the stages of hysteria
through the new art of photography, a suspect practice since patients tended

to perform for the doctors and the doctors to record the patients
who performed the best. But then I do share not only
                    a birthday but a birth year with Felix Cavelliere
of the Young Rascals: "I was feelin' . . . so bad! / I asked my
French family doctor just what I had! / I said Doctuh–Doc-TUH! / Mr.

Charcot–Doc-TUH! / Don' wanna be hysterical . . . no mo'!
Doc-TUH!!" Not much good lovin' in the Freud household,
                    maybe at Chez Charcot, either. Freud marries Martha
Bernays but has little to do with her once she becomes a mother
and then either does or doesn't have an affair with her sister Minna,

depending on whom you do or don't believe. As for Charcot,
there's not even mention of a wife on the more prominent
                    websites. No Betty Charcot or whatever her name was–
Cécile, probably. Jean-Martin and Cécile Charcot invite
you to pitch a hissy fit this Friday afternoon at the famous Salpêtrière

hospital, originally a gunpowder factory that was converted to
a prison for prostitutes and holding tank for the mentally
                    disabled and criminally insane as well as epileptics
and the poor, one of whom was a deliveryman knocked
for a loop in October 1885 and left with partial paralysis, a permanent

headache, and "blank spaces in the tablet of his memory,"
one of which was of the accident itself. Charcot decided
                    the deliveryman's symptoms were a result
of the psychological trauma he had suffered, whereas
the poor fellow's difficulties were obviously the result of brain damage,

of classic closed-head injury complicated by intracranial pressure.
Freud, too, would devote himself to the study of hysteria, but
                    his observations of Charcot's mistaken diagnoses
led him not to confuse physical injury with
the psychological kind but to develop instead his theory of unconscious

symptom-formation or "repression," that walling up
of memories and feelings without which we would not
                    have such ornaments of civilization as art, poetry, music,
and leather underpants. The mind is rather
a snake-pit, isn't it, reader? Especially when it comes to love. There

"he who wants to play the angel behaves like a beast,"
says French philosopher Blaise Pascal. Tristan says
            he'll take Iseult to marry King Mark of Cornwall,
      but in the course of their sea voyage, they drink
a love potion on accident and go at each other like crazed weasels:

      rock the boat, rock the boat, baby, / rock the boat,
don't tip the boat over! And yet there's always Felix Cavalliere.
            Felix Cavilliere says all you need is "Good
      lovin' . . . mmppp mmppp mmppp . . .
good lovin!" I wonder what he meant by that. Scientists don't

      have much to say about love, which is probably for the best—
push any inquiry too far, according to German philosopher
            Karl Jaspers, and "the question no longer pauses . . .
      where it runs into mystery but goes on stupidly to lose
its point by extracting a reply"—though the ones who do brain scans

      of kissing couples say the cerebral cortex goes off during
a juicy kiss like those boxes of fireworks the guys with
            the big stomachs dump out on Mulberry Street during
      the San Gennaro festival and soak with gasoline
and throw a match at, just as the same slurpy, open-mouthed osculation,

      even if unaccompanied by the ear nibbling, fanny patting,
and groin grinding that will ensue, given continued privacy
            and additional alcohol, will send to the brain's pleasure
      receptors such neurotransmitters as norepinephrine,
dopamine, and phenylethylamine, thus simulating the type of brain activity

      you get while distance running, parachuting, and bungee jumping.
Oh, Charcot did say one great thing, which is that "Theory is good,
            but it doesn't prevent things from existing," and since "thing"
      can mean any object, action, fact, circumstance, state of affairs,
deed, event, or performance, it could also mean "kiss," reader, so pucker up.

Why I Don't Drink Before Readings

Because it's as though even a single drop of alcohol
                awakens some area of your brain in which a thought
will begin to take shape the way a mushroom appears
                on your lawn after a heavy rainstorm: one second
        and it's not there, another and it is, though in this case
the thing that is growing in that new area of your brain
                is a phrase you've never heard before,
never even thought of, yet now you're just a heartbeat away

from saying something that no one will understand, not even
                the you who is saying it, yet you know these new words
are on their way to your mouth, that soon you will be saying
                something stupid and almost certainly offensive
        because not only has the new area of your brain opened up
and the words started to take shape in it but also you
                can tell there's also a kind of conduit forming, like
a piece of plumber's pipe that leads through your forehead

and behind your nose until it opens up somewhere
                in the back of your throat, and thanks to some chemical
or perhaps alchemical process or maybe one that has
                to do with bioengineering or evolution or even
        intelligent design, the phrase which left that heretofore unknown
phrase-making area of your brain at a point in time
                that now seems so distant to you, like
the moment when the first man stood up on his legs in the Pleistocene

Era or made the first ceramic pots in the Neolithic,
                has moved steadily since, like a glacier leaving
the ice banks of Greenland and bobbling among
                the other, smaller pieces of ice and the whitecaps
        as it makes its inexorable way toward the shipyards
of Nova Scotia, or, perhaps more appropriately,
                it's chugging along like a little choo-choo train leaving
Manassas Junction, say, or Tchefuncte and heading

for a big city like Chattanooga or Richmond
                or Wilmington, Delaware, only now that phrase
has changed, is now all but unholy, has turned into
                something so horrible that you'll be lucky if anyone
        who hears it ever speaks to you again, though that is no more
going to stop you from saying it than is
                the fact that the dean's wife is sitting in the back
of the room with several members of her book club,

wealthy women who are donors or at least potential
                    donors to your university, your department, your creative
writing program, this reading series, and there they are
                    in the back, and several of them are beaming at you
        approvingly, certain that you are about to uplift
and inspire them with your version of the best that
                    has been said and thought in the entirety of Western
culture, just as your university's vice president

for community affairs is beaming at you, though
                    from the front row, not the back, where she is sitting
with her daughters, two adorable girls of approximately
                    eight and six years of age, and the eight year-old
        is playing a video game, though her sister
is looking around at the room, at the other people, at you,
                    not quite certain why she is there
or what to expect, whether you'll deliver a homily or produce

a musical instrument and play it and sing,
                    has no idea that you are about to look at the far corners
of the room, the one to the left where the bar is
                    and then the other one, where the unused folding
        chairs are stacked, and take a deep breath and let half
of it out and look down at your pages and then up again
                    and open your mouth and say,
"Thank you, thank you so much for that lovely introduction."

JOHN CANTEY KNIGHT

There Are No Aristocratic Vampires

with apologies to Anne Rice

I've lived too long near New Orleans
and grown accustomed to the place.
In the necropolis, there is a silence
among the plastic flowers where
no bees gather pollen. Remembrances
such as these gather spiritual dust.
Light filters through ironwork. Who
are the wealthy dead and of whom
or what are they afraid? Of what use
is fear to the departed? Imported
stone smells vaguely of mountains
in Pennsylvania, Kentucky and Italy.
The chisel has cut deeply names
into this rock that is not of this place
of silt, mud and sand. Granite,
limestone, marble rise from a land
reclaimed by inches from being
muck. In the grand houses of the dead,
they do not hear the mockingbird
move through its repertoire. Silence
sits like the Sphinx, the riddle not
yet guessed. In the vast stone city,
I stroll the avenues and boulevards
past the mansions of the rich whose
names mean nothing to me, only folly.
In my imagination, there are no
aristocratic vampires, only the great
rotting hulk of a thousand Trimalchios.

YUSEF KOMUNYAKAA

from *Requiem*

A thick vein of ink
widens into midnight, into daybreak,
the wind walking Audubon's ghost
through the almost gone, straggly
grass, out into the oily marsh bog
where disappearing land begs no footprint,
out to where hard evidence rainbows
up, leaving thousands hurting to be
counted as nothing more than sea turtle,
eel, brown pelican, egret, mud puppy, crab,
& already water wounds into a slush
of uncountable small deaths moored
in cypress, stinking up Springtime
with a pestilence that goes back to the dark ages
on harbors where boats sway in shifting light,
the dead talking to us from a lost masterpiece,
asking, Where is this, somewhere we are
forbidden to remember, where scavengers
are defeated by what they devour?—
& already from a mile down plumes
keep rising up through night & day,
weeks & months, through animal cries
& the language of robots where
diving machines moon-walk,
surging & falling like drowned shadows
of carrier pigeons clouding the waves,
already. . .

The Leopard

She feels the shape of another animal
three trees ahead, & raises her left front paw.
Dew trembles on each blade of grass
as a snake uncoils among the leaves.
She's a goddess in a world mastered
by repetition & unearthly cadence,
pacing off light hidden in darkness.
She eases down her right paw,
slow as coming to an answer
of the oldest unspoken question.
The prey lifts its sluggish head,
listening for a falling star,
a river running over stones,
& then returns to the hare
half-eaten beside a blooming hedge.
A hundred doors spring open.
A raised paw descends skillfully,
softly. The grass rises behind her.
The mitigated laws of kingdom,
district & tribe do not matter here.
She crouches down inside her
longing, one great leap away
from a wild, simple knowledge.
Sinew, muscle, gratitude—she—
& then to ride another animal
down to growl, tussle, gristle,
& blood-lit veins on leaves left
quivering in the passing night.

Ode to the Saxophone

I've heard men push their thoughts
& dreams into you, making the reed speak
& moan through your shape,
breath so close to a human voice
it says damnation & beatitude.
I know men who've kissed doubt into brass,
& heard each one say, Life,
tear me down to a naked sigh
on a roadside bloody with poppies.
Yardbird, Prez, Trane, Sonny, the Hawk—
you know, I could go on with this roll call
till I am kneeling before the Seventh Son.
I've heard them pour hosannahs,
field hollers, the color of a dress
turning a corner, crying & laughter
in a single note, everything into earth.
Sometimes, only half of what's poured in
comes out. But also I know immortality
can step into a semi-dark basement
at the 2 a.m. blue hour & hug a man.
I've seen them totally illuminated
or barely raised from the dead,
distant cities echoing footsteps.
All the old gospels & curses
are inside this cornucopia
of giving, & all one has to do
is turn you toward a sunset
or spotlight, up to the sky
when he's down.

BILL LAVENDER

For Niyi Osundare

remember the day our
earth became lakebottom
and the sloping lapping shingles
over the eaves our ground

temporary basement
lasting roof

muds and mountains
scrolled that day
a masquerade of fear
in a charmed universe

temporary basement
lasting roof

the time-keeper bird kept silent
the coffin behind the cot
floated out
will it be flow or flood?

temporary basement
lasting roof

a god called olosunta called you wayfarer
seeking the magic gold
to turn hovels into havens
and paupers back into people

temporary basement
lasting roof

instead you found in this country
the clay of your footprints
hierglyphed in molten
lakebottom pap

temporary basement
lasting roof

toe-marks like
watermarks on your paper
the rugged anger of a hunger
for all that was squandered

temporary basement
lasting roof

now it's here in this america
that the golden yam saunters
out of the selling tray
to taunt the famished horses

temporary basement
lasting roof

and in the scheming boardrooms
and power-broker brothels
brigades of tailors already
calculate the mark-up

temporary basement
lasting roof

sometimes when it rains
the poor man's house is beheaded
sometimes when it rains
a mahogany falls across your path

temporary basement
lasting roof

and sometimes when it rains
the earth replies with clover
oh lover of the earth—our earth—
you know what it sees

temporary basement
lasting roof

Honey in the Rock

Can we deny how it blooms
to its own sort of sweetness—
the scraped knee, the insect sting,
the toothsome tears that follow,
then need, fresh as clover
as the child busies us inside
for the salves and bandages,
for hushed words beating from lips
like bee wings brushing petals?

But it doesn't take us long
to taste everything turn sour,
to know even the bees collapse
as all their insides darken
to smoke, to storm clouds, to a comb
of splotches on a radiograph.

Bliss in Our Ten Acres of Pine

In working boots, soles thick as a dead man's tongue,
he climbed down the stand, knuckles white on the last rung,
and when he realized what he would carry home,
his heart leapt, then buckled like the wounded stag.

He wondered if the weather had turned,
his sweat tasting of the sap of a longleaf pine,
his left arm feeling like it had fired the gun,
his fingertip honed to an antler's point.

He knew his wife wouldn't worry enough to call
till his liver sat cold on that night's supper plate.
He could name the hunters able to read the signs,
could list, too, what those men were bound to find:

his truck hunched at the break in the fence line,
a trail of kumquat peels he let fall to the ground,
his face paled to match the birch he fell beside,
the buck's perfect nostrils thrilling with flies.

Inheritance

My mind half-dead in pajamas, the house abed,
my five-year-old suddenly alive as she wonders
about her shabby chic dresser with a family
of roses splayed on the front and each side.
I explain how the hand-me-down came to lean the wall.
Her questions start to gather like junk in a drawer
as her mind arranges all the furniture—
mirror, highboy, kitchen table, chairs,
any piece she hasn't seen us unbox and assemble.

Soon we step through the house's rooms
so I can put to rest how each object ended here.
How a two-story kitchen hutch from the farm
clutches our suburban home's saved jumble.
Two servers, like spinster twins who never split,
why they hover in the corners of the dining room.
How even the poor man's chandelier
that some former owner abandoned here
dangles above us like a pair of earlobes.

Eventually, as we both knew we would,
we end in the darkness of her room
broken by a small light down the hall.
We need no words to slip back in bed.
The quiet pulls away when she asks if I can stay
next to her as night's full length descends.
What can I say about the dark?
It is an afghan handed down through a family
of faces we can't quite place, but recognize.

Many of Us in Our Own

We meander an arch around calm
       water in the dark
to trace movement full moon makes
       above and reflected.

The bayou not deep enough to
       disappear in.
The scattered cypress trunks not wide
       enough for two to hide behind
walking comfortably.

Steps slow and our companions become
       dark whispers in the distance
seen briefly between trees and then
       unseen.

Moon oh, moon oh,
       where'd your momma go?

My sister and I speak solemnly about our hydra
       hearts—the trouble that comes
from love too simple to make molds of.

Moon oh, moon oh,
       where'd your momma go?

A tree that splits by lightning or
       slow persistence, growing toward both
directions of the sky—One trunk toward the
       sun's virgin rays, drunk each morning
fresh, a mess.

One trunk toward the blood of earth worn
       soldier, steeped in heavy light and red, sinks
into bed.

Moon—product of tangled orbits, child
       of planet Thea's pining, spinning,
pining, wanting, collision, rough taste, parts
       dispersed, absorbed into object of
love-lone-earth,

unalone for one brief disaster, dismembered
        forever during violent negotiation
of chemicals, heat of contact, melt, molt, made
        that howling face of white gold too far
away for any father to ever hold.

Moon oh, moon yo'
momma died makin' you.

Sister, my arm perhaps too tight around your
        shoulders as we inch toward the
bayou shore.

We may love ourselves down to places deep
        as death, with metaphor or without.

We step out on top of the water on boardwalk
        planks, moon's reflection surrounds, spotlight
from above and below.

Moon oh, moon yo'
momma died makin' you.

Lay our backs down on smooth wood, begin
        to breathe with every part, with bottom of feet,
with belly, with breasts, with bush, with brow, breathe
        with broad lain planks, breathe
with the tree muscle of beams, begin to
        breathe the pain of missing out of me—to dispel the
face that appears no matter whose arms hold me.

Water arms, water thighs, thoughts
sink and rise, sink and rise, sink and rise.

Try to liken myself to the wood platform I've trusted
        my body to, peaceful and monotonal, until I become
member of a memory from the mind of boards, a longing
        urgent as a child's cry—that boards now shaped and
formed, built suspended over bayou were once tree, connected to
        earth not with piles, cement and nails, but with roots thick
as a mother's arms, thin as a fishing thread.

Water arms, water thighs, thoughts
sink and rise, sink and rise, sink and rise.

Every surface, every cell wall raw rings with some
        unsung something.

Chasing the Onion

We've traveled far in the company of onions.
When Eve received the celestial boot
Her toes came down upon a wicked soil
and up sprang the onion, original bulb,
Puck hopping in all directions.

Wherever early drummers led us out,
onions led out the drummers. At Jericho
some settled and would not move again
for fear of god's attention; and onions nested,
cooking in ashes of a comforting fire.

The Egyptians deified it, carved it on altars.
When the Hebrew children found themselves
fed up with manna, they remembered
the leeks and the onions and the garlic.
But now, they cried, *our soul is dried away.*
They had abandoned a god of many uses
for smoke by day and fire by night, a fire
that would neither cook nor comfort.

Whatever languages, whatever laws
or etiquette, the onion will outlast them.
It's held its own against both lamb and lily,
being itself a lily—the lily of the vulgar us—
perfect for those who long to bite god back.

When each has eaten the other, the rowdy onion
will remain uneaten, roasting in our ashes.
Onion: many layered one, old testament.

Harassed by the Dark Ages

It's not surprising I have Dark Age dreams,
after the books I've read. A frightened woman
is sitting at the edge of the world.
It's early twilight, chilly. Something's burning
farther east, but whether leaves or logs
or community itself, I can't determine;

something's always burning in the past.
This woman has hidden all her words
and only hopes to leave a legacy.
Songs, a story. Letters. That's absurd.
The newest epidemic came with strangers
escaping inland, and soon the usual flood

of Goths will be sludging through the marsh.
The throatless eloquence of fire
will squelch all narrative. She'll plead,
Let me remain myself, if nothing more!
She'll die several ways. I wake depressed
and frazzled. It's a self-indulgent fear,

a series of apocalyptic jimjams
caused by our not-so-Roman peace,
plus living through a freaking hurricane
and flood. I want to beg, *Please, please,
no more anthrax, no more crazy bombers
until my newest book's released,*

*though honestly, I maybe wouldn't mind
if half the Baby Boomers writing poems
caught that long-predicted influenza,
thinning the herd. If there's another storm
the manuscript is stowed in Box 13
at Regions Bank.* Pity the forewarned

who bury their copyrights and silver
under the roots of designated trees,
thinking an oak will last. They'll mourn
and dream of luxuries: identity;
invention; creative self-destruction;
that sweetest of indulgences, complexity.

Archaeology at Midnight

His knees drawn up, my husband lies asleep
so like Tollund Man—the sacrifice
found pickled in a bog. He sinks night-deep
a similar repose upon his face.

Always I've dreamed of archaeology,
the pots and beads that decorate a death;
the gold. Poor health, an inability
to master languages, and general sloth
all kept me back. I also lacked the spleen
for its vendettas: who'd become whose mentor;
the provenance of jumbled figurines;
a major stew about each little splinter.

But in the dark I dream about the altars.
Knossos with the roof off. Newgrange. Malta.

MICHAEL P. MCMANUS

Out There

—For Wayne Magee

Thirty years removed from Saigon,
the living room couch holds
you like a cockpit. The ceiling
fan churns above the room,
its sharp spin an imagined rotor.
Summer heat of the delta
creeps into the house,
flies beat at the screen,
the sun lashes down.
I gather more beer, nearly
frozen from time in the freezer.
You speak of the VA hospital
in Shreveport, the medication
of remembering, past comforts
of alcohol and Asian women.
Slowly the day slithers away,
deeper greens turn to black.
Water buffalo flock the streets,
their headlights flaring on rice paddies.
Looking out the window you tell me,
"buddy it's a war out there,"
and part your hair with bamboo fingers,
each eye glazed to the color of coal.
I say sleep in the spare room
ringed with sandbags and razor wire.
Angry young boys fresh from high school
will patrol the perimeter.
At 0200, after an hour's rest,
I am awakened by the muzzle blast
from shattered beer bottles,
and a drunken voice crouched
in the street shouting,
incoming.

Riding a Horse

Each year when winter set in,
that special season you loved like a daughter,
you filled your pockets with peeled apples
and climbed the pasture fence,

where at sunset you walked the open meadow
over tender clover covered with snow,
to the north stable, a pilgrim's rest,
where you softly clicked your tongue

to the white mare you named Shadow,
who for love of your crepuscular timbre
night after night galloped with you
through driving snow and silent fields.

On wings made from the star's milky light,
you sought the sky and flung yourselves
to far away ridges where you dreamed
of the wind-swept sound of wild horses.

But when that final spring arrived on crutches,
why did you gently caress her trusting mane,
and dare to trust the ice on a melting river?
Mother, you always were such a poor swimmer.

Years later when tending the new orchard,
I heard a neighbor call out at dark,
that you both were a white fire in winter,
who for the simple joy of flight became,

the spark's sudden bursting into flame.

This Far South

No doubt we've all seen
brittle leaves risen from the heap
or swarms of scattered chaff
as breezes work their will over barnyards.
Little comes of such bluster.
A muddle's made from our labor at the rake
when gusts unpetal hedgerows.
Yet there's a moral of sorts
in each brazen raid that snaps the bough
or powerline, topples our bins
to litter the clipped and watered lawns.
For who'd quibble with the spirit
whistling through fence wire? This far south
where coastal trees grow bent,
their stands blanching for brackish winds,
where smoke blown at harvest
hangs a fragrance of burnt cane across the day,
we've all kept watch on weather,
seen gales lay bare our trellised gardens
or clouds let down a dusty funnel in the field.
And nothing can be done
but gather what storms have tossed
and haul the fallen branches to a roadside pile.
This close to the ocean, land's end-most tip,
we tend the ground we've got,
the crops and flowerbeds, mustard plants
and plain rows of parsley that mark our place,
brief though it is, on the tilled and turning earth.

On the History of Syphilis

La peste de Bordeaux, 1497

In this the year of our Lord's harsh grace,
what purge or vestal prayer shall set the biles right again
and quench the wick of fever that sputters in the blood?

Just watch as peddlers bear frictions blent from cinnabar,
a balm of copper flakes for bodies poxed and mottled,
or charms to ward away the ulcerations Venus leaves upon limbs.

Such measures sometimes work, they claim, as will a virgin's kiss
and clyster's worth of wine, yet every Sabbath
brings more stricken who kneel uncured before the cross.

You'll notice teeth loosening around tongues grown puffed
while penitents, with hymns lisped and hosannas half-broken,
show the arm's raw stigmata, flesh marked for the charnel house
where cracked bones forecast our future in their fragile heaps.

And in this the season bees root through each bloom
to plunder sweetness from the field, hover powdered in pollen
as back legs bulge with dusty bundles, there now comes
the barbed retort for all the flux and honeyed glut that gild our days.

We pray, then, dosed with potions while boughs turn ripe
and keepers reap their pails of comb. For here the blest and blighted hour
finds us hobbled to bent attrition, blind in the barren shadow that heaven casts.

My Grandfather's Trees

For years he tended them, mulberry and cedar,
and the crape myrtle squandering its blossoms across the yard—
until he could read each season's passage mapped amid the trees.

Or so it seems to me these days. We often hoisted the dead limbs,
uncoiled the poison vine from cut stumps and fence posts.
One August tent worms wove the oaks in gossamer,
the bridal trunks lovely with spun veils of blight, though all month
my grandfather walked the yard with torches and cans of kerosene.

His was the kingdom where persimmons bent their profligate branches,
and figs, drenched with their own sweetness, rotted where they dropped
so that hornets hung in the grass and bees plundered the honeysuckle.
Most everything went to waste. Mottled pears melted into wet soil
and mockingbirds left plums half-ravaged on the bough.

Yet each summer the attic fan's great blades drew breezes weighted with maypop,
drew in the jasmined evenings to nectar the halls of my grandfather's house
while hard buds of starlight grew luminous among the leaves.
And so the hours conjured their pollen, dusting the fronds of hunched mimosas,
and whole years gave over to hawthorne's cast-off petals and air heavy with honey.

What's left but the language gathered from my grandfather's labor,
that rhetoric of sprawling shade and rainfall, of seasons
ripening thriftless on the stem? For decades he coaxed the slow workings
of root and resin, clipped the stricken branches and banked them for the flames
as blue jays called out their clamorous blessings in the weather.

ROBERT MENUET

Louisiana Sky

I thought the house was settling in the reclaimed marsh;
I've heard this sound before, but never understood
the Louisiana live-oak drops its harvest one by one.
For two weeks now the slow rain comes:
a single acorn hits the roof and bounces, rolls across the slate.

Then another, an hour or a minute later.
Visiting from Richmond, Cousin André brings a letter
from Rouen; our Norman ancestor was no Bovary,
he jokes, but a Viking. He ran the Federal
blockade until the surrender of New Orleans,
and settled with his plunder and his landed bride
on the *Côte des Acadiens.*
In town, he kept Philomene, his octoroon
woman: a blood moon shone upon the magnolia then
in her court of gardenia and hibiscus,
until the day, his fortune
lost, he went where unsilvered neighbors had long before
seceded: to the land of not-forgotten;
and like a cypress branch upon the river he drifted down the days.

From the north, the wind across Lake Pontchartrain
blows moss like pennants in the leafy boughs.
We take down pictures of our parents—
both look away from the old
Norman's plantation of chivalry and dreams, a bubble
broken by nightmares of possession and desire.
My father loved the dark
daughter of a Calcasieu preacher
who refused to wed them; they eloped to the bleeding
oilfields of Oklahoma.
André's mother enlisted in the US Navy, and after Hiroshima she
followed her ensign to Lake Erie's frozen shore. Brother and sister
left the land, but not the burden that they dreamt.

Like little bombs, throughout the night the acorns
fall to earth. And afterwards I dream
that all the old-time senators are discovered

meeting secretly in a long-forgotten
chamber of the Confederate capitol; after 130 years,
a park ranger stumbles upon the living
Jefferson Davis. Vacationers in pastel shirts walk by
the unchanged dreamer and his rebel congress;
he utters nothing, merely sits in his chair like Lincoln's statue,
still as silence and the lingering past.

Free and neutral state

Look down at the damp earth where
the hoof prints impressed one upon the other.
A mineral sledge blocks the way:
on one side its runners dig into the cattle rut
that runs through the meadow
encircled by its curtain of pine.

My father lies unseen in his woodland now,
a memory that will fade and die with me
when no one will remember
the artesian spring he capped
near the deserted slough
where cypress trunks once floated to the mill.

Below Burr's invasion ferry
onto the lawn of dreams and secrets,
there, next to the old rose garden,
the catahoula that survives him
drags a hornless skull;

he worries it all the long winter;
and soon enough
I will collapse
into a pencil point,
a kind of everything
taken
with all I came to understand.

Invited to turn down an empty cup,
I'll fall with clockwork matter into my inner void
before the first wave of tears and noisy starlight,
to join him in some expanding depot
that's not in Rosepine or Longville or New Llano.

The Vision

for my maternal grandmother, d. 1962, Saline, Louisiana

It had been far too long since you had said
"Remember me," the southern covenant,
When in a troubled sleep I stood again
Before the lonely house in which you died
Some twenty years ago, your weak heart broken
By the relentless heat of sixty green Julys.
Beyond fine sands blowing their ghostly roads
Through North Louisiana's pinewood hills,
I saw the pale boards brighten in the sun,
The white and pink oxalis lining the walk
Where bold moss-roses welcomed back the day
And long melancholy summer afternoons
Woke up the four-o'clocks to watch them fade
Into the primrose evening. There, where you lay
With pills and pistol ready by the bed
Listening to sweet gums whisper in the fields
And bobwhites call aloud their human name,
One night, as you had prayed, you died in sleep,
And took your place among the Sudduth graves
Made fragrant by your dignity and grace.
Now you had come: no dream within a dream
But luminous and true, radiant as a source,
Shelling your purple peas, rocking on the porch,
Letting the perfect knowledge of your face
Release me in the calmest depths of love.
You dressed in cotton lavender, of course,
But in a modern style, your spirit's mild
Contempt for time, so quietly expressed.
We did not go inside the darkened rooms
Whose figures moved through half-remembered scenes,
But with your softly wrinkled arm about me
We slowly circled round the house and yard
Seeing each thing as what it truly was,
The old pecan cocooned in dry June skies,
Crape myrtle great with bees and dragonflies,
Measureless wells, so lucid in their noons!
No fantasy's compensatory lie

Or image drawn at random from the flow,
You were the angel summoned up in pain
That innocence might walk upon the earth's
Envisioned ground, by memory sustained.
At last our circle closed, but as you stopped
And I awoke to consciousness and tears,
You said, "It'll be all right," words whose truth
Is all we crave, the voice of providence.
You sat back down beside your peas and flowers,
Smiling, talking, laughing, singing aloud
But to yourself alone, there, where you wait
And think of me until I too can go
Into the only world the heart would ever know.

JEN J. MOODY

Mama never measures

when she cooks
(except for rice).
Everything comes
in pinches of pepper
and shakes of spice,
an extra flick
of the wrist
for *lagniappe.*

When our family was whole
every meal was hers,
not feasts but comfort—
in smothered chicken,
red beans and rice, gumbo,
jambalaya.
She put emotion
in every portion,
for her children
(and wayward husband).

Her small and quick hands
chopped green onion
and celery, cordless phone
held between ear and shoulder,
calling her little sister to ask
is it a half onion or a whole,
cher, whatchoo rememba?
I watched her from the kitchen table,
math homework unfinished
because Daddy wasn't home
yet. He's on a business trip,
she would tell me. *I'll help*
you, bebé, as soon as I'm done
a-cookin'.

And she always did,
after she let me taste her creations,

the flavors sparking on my tongue.
Years later I would cook
exactly as she did, hoping
to find some hidden secret
inside sausage, a skill
within bouillon cubes,
the ability to keep on
after he walked out the door.

I haven't yet mastered
the art of marrying food with feeling,
though I know the trinity
(celery, bell pepper, onion),
I know to splurge
on a good gumbo pot,
and I know that when I cook,
my clumsy hands
slicing sausage,
the steam is some spirit—
maybe hers—locked in my kitchen.

GEOFF MUNSTERMAN

Resurrecting Fish & Other Mysteries

1.

An incision from gut to gill makes a mouth
where words are innards spoken to the grass.
My bare toes smitten in grime wiggle & chirp
like wind-chime. Tonight childhood returns:
bare feet creasing weeds as cicadas simmer.
Quick handiwork evades stink. So freshly dead,
eyes warble & twitch with water's harsh stars.
This place is tar or marsh. Oil or soil. Derrick
or delta: it has never had to choose. A kind land
yielding crop and fuel favors neither & creatures
survive despite industry's humidity scorching sky.
Men wake early & work. Even the thumbless
among them lift crab traps at dawn. Filet for pay.
Even blind men row toward something of worth.
Directionless, they row forward. Grown up now
we know don't trust the crickets singing all hours.
Their nighttime hollers merely death row brogues.

2.

Sometimes night is a horny teen nibbling lobe.
His skin Shinola, his manners shit, & don't know
whether to scratch his watch or wind his ass.
Cooks a mean plate of fish. Skillet hissing like
liquid from logs, its flesh hardens with flavor.
Bones fiddled clean. Post-meal preaching ends
when Leo Woolverton, drunk at the fire, singes
his ass hairs mooning the shy girl's shier cousin.
After laughing hard enough for tears, all blame
these dirty hunters can muster is lost in cheap
beer, hot fish, and the shiny cheeks of shy girls—
their compassion pried with stories of the past.
A fish this big. A storm so foul. The once upon
performance of a ritual no shaman recommends.
Spoken only hushed. What bones not choked on
by beagles are released back to the current. No
flesh, no blood, no scales & yet become a fish again.

Detour to New Orleans, September 2005

The route unfamiliar, the destination home.
Once I'm through Ohio, I'm pushing eighty
until a patrolman in Tennessee flags me down.
He sees Louisiana plates and lets me go.
Boots my father gave me keep the pedal down.
To go the old way means seeing other states
whose homes were torn to kindling:
Huntsville to Birmingham, Birmingham
to Meridian, Meridian to Hattiesburg,
Hattiesburg until you hit New Orleans East
where all that stands is Mary Queen of Vietnam—
a church my father built.

Each town I pass through weeps with me
for the city where I'm heading to.

Sleepless weeks in Ohio watching news:
the levees failing, the phone lines down.
Grandpa's mind lost ten months back
when father died; Grandma stubborn.
The girl who'd hitched a ride that summer
surely drowned, or in the Superdome.

A teacher tells me if I'm late again,
she'll drop me from the class.
All the poems of mine she's read
and it's a student asks about my home.
It doesn't matter. All I want to do
is get back home to see if it's still there,
then turn around to the life I'd been making,
unaware a storm could knock it down.

KAY MURPHY

for my Books

I wouldn't know how many books I lost
if not for Ryan, twenty-three, who'd drawl
he owned more than two thousand. I recall
the other students owned twenty at the most
and indicated he had double crossed
them. But I became determined, before fall
semester (even though I'd have to crawl
through attic boxes) I'd count mine; then I'd boast.

Salt mud, filthy, soaked the bottom rows, gummy
black pages. Higher up, the mold embossed
the first edition hardbacks. That stunned me—
to save twelve, see three thousand others tossed.

Behind the bookshelves is what still appalls:
such beautiful black roses on white walls.

Eggplant

They droop from leaves the size of elephant ears,
white bulbs flowing from lilac flowers,
capped green sockets, purple-streaked at first
and turning sunward. These nightshades,
the manor of Bella Donna—deadly poison
named for a beautiful woman—possess
pale pulpy flesh, seeds, and skin
the color of sorrow and Lenten passion.
Yet they make a festive caponata or ratatouille.

Oh, aubergine, heavy as a baby's bottom
when ripe, what have you to do with penance
or pained souls in purgatory? Your color only
suggests contrition. Still you mirror mystery:
growth of seed from the uterus of soil,
sunlight's gestational warmth and incubation;
mornings and evenings rise and fall,
awaken and silence birds—the old arousal
of life and downward spiral to night.

Oyster Shuckers

Their names are no longer familiar.
There was Mack and Sleepy and Claude,
at whose home I spent hours.
My brother must remind me about Eviste,
Lucius, and August, the one who ate
only bananas for lunch and napped
on the concrete floor of my father's shop.

Once he told a woman the oysters
weren't good, unsalty and too small.
She was stupid, he said, to purchase
oysters like that. Vanished now,
with the oyster dressing made from New Orleans

170

French bread, airy and light, and the Fridays
when my father brought home from his shop
a pint to dip in cornmeal and fry—
oysters the shuckers had opened.

Revisiting New Orleans in a Season of Joy

"I knew I had to come home. It was a matter of time."
Mona Lisa Saloy, The Times Picayune, December 26, 2007

I

How could I forget the rooflines of tile,
the details of plaster gargoyles embracing
interior walls? Seven years scarred
with deaths and flood, and I am home again
amid these scenes and familiar scents,
the years peeling away my fears,
imagination's false claims. A sluice gate
opens to streams of tears and their sister joy.

Out Gentilly Boulevard past the ruins
of Elysian Fields, our stucco house appears
smaller than I recall. On Bruxelles off Broad
the grocery store my great uncle owned
has disappeared. Lakeside, the university
mushroomed, swelling structures everywhere.
I can no longer locate where I officed or schooled.
Only the mansions along St. Charles remain.
Memories rise like smoke of yesteryear.
I shiver and curl up against the cold.

II

Before the museum, the oaks have vanished,
replaced by slim stalks with auburn leaves.
Two exhibits depict the pain of Katrina,
Rolland Golden paintings and the art of children
displaced and lost, working their grief and fears
into crayon drawings. Frames of destruction
will play for years in their memory's films.

Amid pouring rain, a squadron of ducks
align at equidistant paces across the road.
A straight edge of blue bills to warn us
to flee before the waters again drown the city?
Is this how they acted when the levees broke
and the lake crafted her month-long tides?

III

Before and after, there is hope: in the Quarter,
at Café Degas, ripe with meals to tempt the palate:
pompano with lemon-caper risotto, yam and tasso
soup, golden croissants and quiche, special treats
of coffee and beignets. Pleasures of the tongue
and flesh, of friendship renewed, recumbent
as leaves folded by winds, lifting us beyond
what we believe we know or understand.

JAMES NOLAN

Over the Oysters

for Lee Grue

Bobby Blue Bland wipes
beads of sweat from his brow
with a big blue handkerchief
then drapes it over the mike
while back in a far corner
we have burst out crying—
birth death marriage divorce
failure success money sex—
waiters tilting to us tray
after tray of half shells
and pitcher after pitcher
of Dixie beer because here

in New Orleans feelings
are cheap and raw and opened
and we eat them by the dozen,
weeping like the Walrus
and the Carpenter over life
because we are living it,
weeping over the oysters
as one by one we swallow them,
the sea finally paying attention,
its own tears arranged in a circle,
each broken as a secret locket
and smiling slowly, we drown

as Bobby Blue Bland mops
his face, stares straight
into the spotlight
and belts out one more song.

King Midas Blues

We have prayed for
the power. Now it's ours.
Everything we touch
turns to smudge.

From the Alaskan coast
to the Gulf of Mexico,
everywhere we go
turns to sludge.

From the exhaust-pipe air
to the flaming oil wells
on our Iraqi victory cake,
every horizon blurs to smog.

BP gold, Texaco gold,
dolphins and pelicans,
the turtles in the bayou
are slick with black gold.

Golden-haired, our most
loved daughter lies dying
of cancer at twenty-six
with petrochemical cells.

We have killed for
the power. Now it's ours.
Everything we own
turns to poison.

Acts of God

Outside, rowboats paddled up Canal Street
while I was delivered howling by lantern
in a hospital called Hôtel Dieu during
a hurricane that knocked out New Orleans.
I have a feel for rattling window panes,
for rivers racing through sky, for heaven

flung endlessly down. This year August ends
with God banging on the door like the police.
Venetian blinds clatter against glass,
gusts ripple through calendar pages back
to the day of my birth, the steel wok hung
by a hook from the rafter chimes an Angelus

against the skillet, curtains billow as I
follow from bed to bed, room to room, city
to city, continent to continent, capturing
the wind like a spinnaker, covering weather
maps with cyclonic swirls and arrows, over-
flowing boundaries, sexes and time zones.

My kitchen globe brightens as the sky blackens
and rising with the steam of a boiling kettle
I approach my glory, the air finally matching
my emergency, reaching for the same velocity,
announcing ourselves with a loosened shutter
back and forth against the side of the house.

Claiborne and Toledano

We are standing near the corner of Claiborne and Toledano staring at a cat we have just coaxed onto the seat of a makeshift bench nailed to a tree. The pack of dogs has finally disappeared. They were reluctant to leave the cat they had trapped balancing against the tree on the top inch-wide rail of the bench. They had taken turns, one dog switching off, hunting like dingoes. I look around again, make sure no one's circling us. There's another couple on the corner waiting for the bus, talking, joking. Though I know they didn't stop to save the cat, they make me feel better. Their laughter makes the dogs seem unreal. The cat is still sitting sphinx-like on the bench, staring in the direction the dogs disappeared, unwilling to move. His back legs are soaked in his own urine and somehow this makes him human to me. I don't know what to do. Headlights shine from behind me. I turn to face the car that has pulled up. I am not relieved to see the lights on top, the cop stepping towards us. He's stopped only because we're white. I look for the other couple standing on the corner, but the bus has come and gone, taking them away. There is no one else around. What's the problem? Do you know where you are? Do you know that's the Magnolia Projects right there? I think about my expired brake tag, expired license plate and turn to walk away. The cat, too, has disappeared.

BILJANA D. OBRADOVIC

Life's Little Disruptions

for Radiclani Clytus

My colleague gave me a ride home from work,
but refused a drink, as he had to pick up his wife.
Later, the second time this week, someone stole
his car, even with its battery disconnected, even
after he had stolen his own car back, having found it
a few blocks from their apartment in the 9th Ward,
historical, predominantly black neighborhood,
now disrupted by affluent white gays and lesbians
where dealers sell crack, where at night he watches
his neighbors carry "borrowed" TVs, VCRs, PCs,
near the place he and his wife had to move
away from, around the corner, to have needed heat,
where he had to kill a rat or live with it;
so now he comes to work by cab
hoping the insurance money will suffice
for a new car, or with luck to steal his car
again, then sell it, to double his money. Why not?

Today, a Bosnian Moslem or Croat refugee cab driver
chatted with him, then wrote some words in my language
on a piece of paper, without letting him know what they meant,
without letting him know his name, or why he was here
in New Orleans so far from the bloodshed,
to give the words to me—a Serb; my curious black colleague
handed them to me—I blushed, not understanding
why he'd hand me this note with
"Fuck you! You're a cool pussy!" on it.
Once he explained, I understood.
Ethnic hatred has reached me again.
My innocent, caring friend, understood as well;
both of our lives disrupted, our fates united
in these ugly words of hatred,
away from our homes we fear our own.
I go home and find a mouse on top of my stove.
Do I need to move too? I can't kill it.
I can't live with it. There is no answer.

Dead Man Floats

This is how it is done.
The face stares down.
The eyes look down into
what has drowned it.

It is all like a puzzle now.
That piece of wreckage
there, or that fragment
of memory, almost gone, too.

The arms stretch out
as if the body were
flying, or spinning,
but had lost all direction.

That is the magic of
now becoming so detached,
that neither sky nor
earth would claim the skin.

The bones spread themselves
into a new constellation
in another space that
only the winking and

pouting fish would admire.
The heart floods with water.
The thoughts slap
together like waves and

try to push across time,
as if there were a shore
anywhere, but infinity has
withdrawn its offer.

Hurricane and Its Eye

after Katrina

They say I'm calm here
at this center where my winds
don't blow and my sight
down to the earth stays clear.

They say my thoughts should
turn philosophical now as I
think over the devastation
I have brought: houses gone,

trees uprooted, shores
ragged and lacking definition.
And that now is the time
for me to see the advantage

of order over the chaos I prefer,
to think about the harm
of my reckless speed, the
wayward path of my strength.

They say this insight here
will lead to regret so that
I won't punish the living
anymore and won't try to

rearrange what was fixed.
I'm to call off the trouble
still building in my dark clouds,
as if I could reason with

my angry and turbulent winds,
but I say I can't collect
my wild thoughts or tame
the outer terror that claims me.

Tell About the Trees

after Gustav

downed in a big wind,
their branches that crack
loose in pain and their
frightened leaves that shudder.

Or is it that their leaves
gasp as they twirl, or
is it that they scream?
Then that crash is the same,

isn't it, whether the trees
hit the ground and make
the dust jump, or whether
they smash the roof and

old tiles fly away from
what they were to protect?
Then the roots, you say,
tell about the roots,

twisted and up in the air,
practicing their own deadly
dance, and tell about
the trunks then broken or

split because their weight
punishes them, and the gravity
that destroys their balance.
Tell about what's left

under those trees, you keep
on saying, tell what chance
there is for survival when
trees become the angels of ruin.

The Fisherman and the Evening News

His mind freezes. He mumbles
something about our old argument
over Barataria Bay and boat repairs.
I tell him to turn the damn thing off.

Oil sheen glosses over his eyes.
He says the sour bile in his stomach refuses to gush.
Brief flit of speech and his muscles go slack.
When his gaze fails to reflect me,
his wall stands complete.

We hear about the whales and dolphins.
Crude shining like a crow's wing,
tar washed up like poisoned licorice,
plumes of false gold drown brown pelicans.

A child's careful drawing
of oil-stained earth shakes him.
He gathers nets at his feet,
returns to mindless mending.

Before I change the channel, a sign flashes:
No More Oysters in New Orleans Parish.

Lure

At midnight we canoe the bayou
in a yellow shell, a daffodil petal

curling into dark. Only now
I begin to know this man,

his beard and nails' blunt
manicure. He tells me the red

eyes of alligators sweep cypress
knees bald, how the animal

leaps vertically if provoked.
He asks for his harmonica. I lean

over, steady myself on the frame.
His notes lap the hyacinth,

burrow in the brown mud.
He tells me the animals come

for marshmallows. *Why didn't I bring
a bag? Why am I always forgetting?*

Months ago, he told a waitress
to lower her voice—

its timbre hurt his ears. She laughed,
thought it a joke. Now we knock

our wooden oars. Up front,
under tupelo, he points

to scarlet breaks in the shadows,
rips a mallow flower

from a bush, crepes it
across the water's copper finish.

Water

How can we own a thing that travels
Constantly, evaporates, clouds over,
Rains back and pools,
                  or else sinks,
Each fold or fault distorting its movement
In ways no sense of gravity predicts?
And how can we know the lateral habits
Of water, an immigrant who cannot
Settle anywhere, but circles over
Landscapes, erodes every border,
Edges shorelines of immeasurable sand?

Etched banks can channel it,
The current cutting deeper down,
Driving itself from underneath,
No longer water then but the force
Of gravity gathering its weight.
A watershed deflects the rain,
Or water table drops from use,
The downhill graduals of streams,
Spring floods and overflowing dams—
All tributaries feeding down
Into one long revisionary river
That curls against itself as if
The only way to move ahead
Was by deflecting back,
Like a language that explains itself,
A story told,
              this time about water.

The Vegetable Garden

Needled by death for change, for simple change,
We turn the soil,
                    another season's crop
Growing from seed, from rain and last year's rot
Into a fruit we never arrange:

The lettuce outgrows our appetite,
While fences smother with towering beans
And tomatoes swell from the dark of their roots;
All tactile reaching for decay turns green

And hangs in the spray of a garden hose.
Dripping with light, the leaves must bow,
Darkening under shadows we cast
Walking among each picked, each weeded row.

Seasons are canned into lines among shelves,
Are named and dated while vinegar boils,
Filling the house with an acrid smell,
And vines are turned beneath themselves:

Our garden is a form that answers cost,
And, growing out of hand with constant care,
Distinctions bloom, ripen, rot, and bear
Into the gathering grasp of something lost.

The Name

With an easiness we almost learn . . .
Like the isolated shadow of a palm
Or variegated light by which a fern
Casts the lattice of its green calm—
Two workers lift in place a new fountain
For the courtyard in the starched hotel
Where, retired, my parents visited and remained.
Now, there's little here of them to tell,
Except that they were happy spending
Their days in shops, or walking the battery
When evenings cast outlines of the ending
They treated with such baroque finality.
Old clothes outgrew them, though their profiles changed
As imperceptibly as the courtyard
Where, year after year, they still arranged
Small gatherings and monitored
Their guests like two strict preservationists.

For years they did the ordinary thing—
The suburbs in a haze, high hedge and smoke
From cigarettes and grill, bluffed twinings
Overhead, rising beyond the jokes,
Choked laughter, and descending ice
Poured from lilting pitchers. . . premium gin
Precise as medicine.
                          And twice,
Promotion or market up—some win—
The two of them waltzed across the patio
Laughing, we children laughing, not knowing why,
As the afternoon turned evening like a slow
Fade-out under a canvas sky.
There was a game we played in which
One child held a flashlight and one a mirror,
Attacker and attached, the switch
Coming when, angled just right, the mirror
Blinded back, and then the game reversed.
I think our parents played that way,
But differently, more slowly, and with words.
It was their means for setting things to stay,
Not out of differences or change
But somehow from the names they played
Back to one point—each view exchanged.

What brings me to this hotel now
Is a kind of stalled curiosity
Opening out the way a pattern goes
From holding its geometry
To something wider.
                              Crisp habits raise
Their own squared world, but lack
The final fact, when every gaze
Becomes the other view. The child
Looks up and back, then looks ahead
Beyond his own eroding ground, wild
As a nightmare's cranking landscape of the dead,
Where he calls the names he knows but no one wakes.
There water is the only constancy;
It fills headlong whatever way it takes,
Channeling a deep redundancy
As it steadies where its banks divide
Wider with floods, higher with drought.
For me that landscape was the side
Of a failing wall, a fountain's spout
Widening as I listened to regret
Coiling and uncoiling like a chain
Linking everything it touched. It let
Me stand once, balanced like a name,
Realizing that the water fell by rising,
And that what it brought and took away were the same.

JULIA RAMSEY

Pretty Bones

What's inside our sutured skin
doesn't seem much the concern of aesthetic. To pay
a compliment to a face: charming, despite all
accountable to chance genetics, flesh's coarse grace.
A compliment to pretty bone
is offputting—but why? I find it hard to see

the difference between beauty and beauty, hard not to see
the skeleton sliding under a man's skin:
straight femur, the cusp of hip-bone
curved like the place where the fawn nestles. We pay
our respects to the dead, grace
their graves with rotting flowers, with no regard for all

the detritus inside: a body's olive-pit in its altogether—
fallible flesh fallen away, naked for the dark to see.
To be spindled, hard, specific-white: state of grace
uncovered by time's peeling-back of skin
and fat. Sooner or later flesh's bill must be paid,
its grease-flame gutters while underneath the bone

sings, quiet and shining, a bony-
knuckled fist raised in protest of all
temporary. Twenty-four columns curved, Adam less one, payment
and bride-price. The body's history seen
in flesh's scarred map: at twelve I skinned
my knee down to white patella, sticky-red. (Never very graceful.)

In the reliquary, Saint Magnus' proximal phalanges grace
Ursuline Cathedral; the ascetic bone
still, dimpling the skin
of the quiet. If you could gather all
the relics in an armful, they'd assemble, you'd see
a skeleton slinking down State Street, paid

up in concentrated jingle-jangle holiness. He pays
a tip of the hat to swooning nuns, "Sister Agnes, Sister Grace,
you're looking well this morning I see—

oh no, can't complain, these old bones
don't fire up the way they used to, but all
I can say is how happy I've been since I lost that skin."

On cloudy evenings, you can see the round bone
of the sun: a graceful, half-obscured circle, all
its radiance in the pay of cirrus' thin skin.

MARTHE REED

Of the Marsh Arabs: Shamiya

That old reeds and fresh reeds should grow
in the reed-beds: may An not change it.
—Lament for Sumer and Urim (Ur) c. 1950 BC

An expanse of light recalling water, palm trees thick with fruit. There is nothing analogous: an expression of certainty. I am astonished

Such words forge affinities

Blue body and gold air. Like willows or tamarisks. The Shamiya flickers in birdsound. At once luminous and blurred

Gold abstracted against blue

Light stipples the air. Is gold. Idiom of warblers or reed thickets. Collapse of day. Is there such a thing?

Water composes a relief of sound and shade

Narrow wake, flight of darters. Reed shelter. *Shamiya* demands the correct use of the expression "to see". Floating realm

Certainty excuses itself

Against the fall of day, such propositions erode. Meander of ibis and marbled teal. White-fronted geese among reeds. Rivered ground

Later, we are astonished

RACHEL REISCHLING

Triptych

We met in Paris. Arias shimmered from my head
like goldleafed halos on smiling madonnas.
Now nothing, like crocuses, blooms
   as your hand reaches across

space and time (across the wood-planked
table) to offer me soft French cheese.
You remember an apple. You remember teaching.

Molding. I remember picking: at birch bark, at skin—
at dead things.
In the beginning you created heaven, I, the earth.

Paradise was a blue sign with an arrow pointing
right, toward Saint Chappelle,
your comfortable silence, our two

pension beds, pushed together.
In the afternoon, we're back to find (as prophesied)
our bed pulled back apart, pillows fluffed,

new sheets, starched and tucked in tight.
Little cleaning hands erased all evidence
of our divinity. Who could guess

we were anointed,
were gods, omnipotent with champagne,
and full of love for all the world?

BRAD RICHARD

Dirt-Dauber's Nest

A hollowed hump of mud
built on my bathroom windowpane,
shaded by pine branches.

There's the hole
the wasp hunched herself through,
her thousand frugal motions shaping
smooth dimensions of a dim interior.

Morning after morning, I heard her
thump and rap against the glass
as she hauled her fractions of earth,
daubed and molded them, haven-making.

So much intention
perceived in a thing so small.
Her business done, she disappeared,
leaving no larvae seething there.
Summer thickened every living cell,
but her work spawned no swarm
gorging itself at the azalea's mouth,
no builders of other nests.

It clings, sterile, to my bathroom windowpane.
Nothing lives or dies there.
Nothing haunts or wants it,
just a socket of earth and air.

More than instinct, less than sentiment,
something keeps me from scraping the window clean.
I go on doing what I do.

Mere wind hisses in the pines,
empties itself through my house.
Whatever inhabits me at this moment
goes on doing what I do.

The Cooling Board, 1929

He tried to ask someone what happened
                    to the back of his head, but the words
                                    fell apart in his mouth and got caught

like stones in his throat, and he ended up here
                    in his one good shirt and a friend's old suit.
                                    June, but it's cool where he is, laid out

on a woven cane mat stretched taut
                    in a folding frame over a block of ice,
                                    the whole getup tented in silk.

But no one ever told him what happened,
                    not his friends who carried him in,
                                    not the undertaker who slicked his hair

over the rut left by a steel rod that shot
                    like an arrow when a gas still burst a pipe
                                    right when he was leaning in to check it—

the refinery's paying for the funeral.
                    If you cared to look in his wallet,
                                    you'd find a pretty girl's picture

inscribed *for my "Spindletop,"* and another,
                    clipped from the *Port Arthur News*, of a whale
                                    seventy feet long, beached at Sabine Pass—

that would have been a story to tell!
                    The ice sweats a slow fever in its pan,
                                    and weird dew on his cheek makes runnels

through rice powder and rouge, and the words
                    finally settle, down low in his windpipe.
                                    Would you believe he grew up on a rice farm

outside Gueydan? That he loved the smell of asphalt
                    on his skin when he woke? Well, that's all over.
                                    But lift the drape and he'll tell you what it's like

now in his palace of jacquard and ice.

I Take a Book from the Shelf

Infinity and the Mind
        and shards of glass fall out

so I'm back in the tornado
        crouched with my husband
                and the dog in the hallway

while wind seizes the house
        shatters windows and rips
                the roof away   tarpaper tossed

flapping across the freeway
        so I'm back with my mother
                when her truck's impact flings

the deer through the windshield
        and onto her chest   slivers
                in her hands for months

and when I land I'm back
        in my father's flooded studio
                I'm ruined canvas I'm smashed plates

but if I shut my eyes   I'm safe
        in the car with my husband
                crossing the parish line at the canal

crossing the bridge   dropping
        from lit suburbs into the dark
                of drowned neighborhoods

our headlights picking shards
        from this chaos inside me
                that doesn't care where I live

Hot with Mosquito

Seeking through
thick layers of
sticky Louisiana night,
close after full moon
with pack of stray dogs
headed East
sniffing.

Two vanloads of Mexicanos
stopped in the parking lot
of a gas station shadowed down,
humming like big cicadas,
droned in velvet tone,
flashing gold teeth
and the whites of
tropical eye.

Down the street,
rowdy small town boys
raucous with pick-up truck
and too much beer,
laughter like bubbles
too heavy to float.

Dark trees back away
from the road with
who knows what beyond.

It's hot with mosquito
and no wind.

GEORGE F. RIESS

Macondo

On April 20, 2010 the BP Macondo oil well
in the Gulf of Mexico exploded, killing
eleven crew members immediately and gushing
out of control for many months afterward.

1.

Awake at dawn with black chicory we waded
the piling that tethered the boat and hoisted over
the gunnels. Bobby Magee popped the Evinrude,
puttered us out to drop our nets a dozen
in line in the channel, and in bare light
we barely made the floats on our first run.
He cut the motor 20 feet before
my silent hands underwater on
the cotton cord pulled and set the net.
Then hand over hand I hauled the agony
of our catch to the surface til three barnacled
crabs broke, gaping claws snapping
a last gasp of brine. Down the line
a quarter mile and back, two and three crabs
per net, we filled a hamper and puttered back.

2.

The marsh is soft at dawn, a place of birth,
a fecund lady delicate in an expectant
way, sibling creatures cycling in
and out of her grasses and still water.
Shy and parthenogenic, she needs nothing,
only to be left alone, like heaven, to yield
her secrets only to the angels with nets and traps
who have come and gone for generations.

3.

But the Gigolo sells himself by the hour
to politicians trolling for kick-backs,
johns trading tax breaks, taking turns on their knees.

195

And he peddles his science as safe.
So the reckoning. Eleven souls in hard hats
incinerated, instant ash. An ocean
of fish bellied up, as inside out
as the puking well. Pelicans tarred and feathered
blinking oil black in their eyes.
Another scene in the geocide.

4.

The lost world. Cacophony of seabirds
in their morning scrum for scraps.
The slap of a tethered skiff in syncopation
with the surf. The strain of oars in the stroke against
the Gulf. The chapel of cypress, branches vested in robes
of moss, impenetrable in diurnal darkness.
A boiling court bouillon, cayenne bay leaf mustardseed,
baptizing blue crabs red. And the salt wind,
all the help the seawall needs to stand
upright a man bent by the daily dread,

the lost world. Kingdom come and gone.

Summer

And we'll all be together again.
On summer nights in a jasmine life
we settled the porch in white wicker chairs
and spoke about nothing anyone ever
remembered. We chatted in the chatter
of Southern cicadas, trading secrets and gossip,
and talked with more ease than we listened:
of widows sipping sherry on hot afternoons,
handsome husbands having all night affairs,
housewives having nervous breakdowns,
snug in our woven white wicker.

And we'll all be together again.
On summer nights in a sweet olive life
we lay like feathers on white washed sheets
in the lullaby of ceiling and oscillating fans.
Our yellow dog chased a mallard in the marsh,
thighs and paws flexing in his goose down pillow
asleep in the sleep only dogs understand.
With bedroom screens luffing like sails,
we tacked out of time, rolling and pitching,
our dreams at the tiller washed out of recollection.

And we'll all be together again.
On the St. Charles line the trolley will stop
for each in his turn to board as they were
at the age of their choice and dressed in style,
our big-breasted grandmothers in thatch roof hats,
our double-breasted grandfathers with gold chain watches,

our mother and father so handsome again,
and with aunts, uncles, brothers and sisters,
we'll sing a sad song to all that is gone
that will never come again, to all
that was said and the promises made
that never came to pass. We'll
ride once more to the end of the line,

And we'll all be together again.

Regarding Dr. Gachet

"I have a portrait of Dr. Gachet with the heartbroken
expression of our time."
                   – from a letter from Vincent to Theo van Gogh

His head is eclipsed by the moon
of his white cap. The bells
of the flowers beside him
ring peals of cleaving.

Should the fissures of heart
be pried wide? What god
to appease: mind or art?

My lover, who wears no
white cap, hides his lacunae,
though rents and tears are just
visible beneath his frayed sleeves.

If you would reach towards his brow,
he'd pull back, rejecting the small gesture
as too sentimental for him, like
the foxgloves on the table
and the doctor's golden hair.

The expression of Dr. Gachet's heart
can be no different from ours:
it's one of hubris or pathos or joy
in a gravity of longing.

DAVID ROWE

Salamander; or, Splitting the Word Asunder

To get out of its way
& let the word have its say;
to allow salamander,
with its ballistic tongue,
to speak as it were
for itself. . .

ssssSeethes forth from between
parted lip-flesh the steam,
the humid heat,
to hiss the wheel, the *salamandala*, into motion.

Sa: natural exhalation
made conscious mantra
via the Tibetan lama's
art & concentration;
seed syllable born ready to spill
& to spell its semen-antics.

Sa-*la-illaha-illa-allah*-mander

Sal: first step of the blessed meanderer,
samana en desultory route to salvation;
Philosophic salt, it aggravates
our thirst for experience, which is to say: heartbreak.

Saltatory salmon of wisdom which
puts fire in the poet's belly,
the Promethean liver, iron-rich
& ever nourishing the birdsoul.
Then again, the homeopathic salve, salicylic acid,
flame-fighting febrifuge.

Sala: inside-out "Alas," sigh
of affirmation-in-spite
-of-everything, a solemn cry
of mercy realized as grand merci,
universal love chosen as armor
by the jilted paramour.
Maya's cherry which secretly

bears the stone-seed of Buddhahood,
sal-*om-mani-padme-hum*-ander.

Salam/Shalom-Ander: a benediction: "Peace-to-Man;"
passionate man of peace
amidst passion's holocaust,
Word on the cross, Word in the manger.

Sa-*la-illaha-illa-allah*-mander

Salome: ekstatic maenad, tender
-hearted wetnurse & blood-crazed render,
strip-dancing the shamanic mandate,
at each of hell's seven almond-shaped gates
shedding a veil until she's translated
to the Muses' Mount Helicon
having made vulnerability
her most venerable ability,
having forged her foibles into fables,
beheading the ego—"*Sauft alle mit einander*"—
& thereby midwifing the death-in-life/life-in-death cycle.

Soolam: black stone which proves pristine dream pillow & golden
ladder to heaven & back.
Sal ammonica: piss & dung of pilgrims' camels
refined into life-promoting fertilizer, rebel's
& reveler's explosives, smelling salts to awaken consciousness.
Sacred/Taboo Untouchable, Outcast destined to cast out our sins & demons.

A la the dervish performing his turning (*sema*),
the salamander is the genius of emptiness (*sama*)
generating wings & taking flight (samara), finding
purchase in the doorway of King
Solomon's Temple.

Sa-*la-illaha-illa-allah*-mander

I am
I am that
I am that I am.
The highest cause of everything is living
within the thing itself,
verdant word as wheel & whirler of the wheel,
Dharma-chakra come full circle back to mysterious "S,"
death-tree shading Zeus' birth-cave, amphibious
alphabetic agent both of hissing demise & of plurality:
ssssSalamanderSsssss.

WILLIAM RYAN

Where to Begin

You observe from a distance the sea
at the brink of suburbia—and in the sky,
escaped headlights, three bright points
on a vertical plane. You observe
by moonlight the times tables
spinning in a simple cosmology,
which you understand almost completely.
You observe phosphorescent organisms,
each of their feet in a cell of salt water,
pitching forward lyrically every seven
seconds with the rotation of a low-impact
microwave antenna. Your head grows
a foot sadder, like a glacier and a sea
mammal, too fraught to levitate with hope,
too far gone for trick language, and
from your soul, which, you observe,
has the wingspan of a housefly,
comes an image: cherubic little twits
holding up electric lights, benign
mathematics tangled in the border work,
and in the detail, two words sadder
than one, three words that misrepresent
the world, no word that is not another
mistake, word nailed on top of word.

To dissect the wrist to learn more
about the hand—this isn't funny.
To call the heart *heart* and the brain
brain isn't funny. To cleave light
into color isn't funny, revealing the lack
of simplicity prismed in a drop of dew.
Or to begin again, stubbornly, with the whole
body, including all the apocryphal
translucent parts and all the thoughts
in the heart and in the body (which
is a larger heart, beating openly,
brave and vulnerable) and remain
nothing, with small bravery, and

something, after all, with more bravery—
this isn't funny—and how would you know
when to stop laughing, as the human
clapper of the bell, the upside down
smile of the face, at the club's joke
to the bone, at the killing jokes,
at the history of killing jokes,
as the man who wandered dumb
into the animal, poor thing?

And then where to begin
again, on cue, during the commercial
at the brink of suburbia, at the passing
of the first clear water, at the third sex
of torture, Latin roots emerging
all over the mouth? And what is
the third sex of torture
like? Like the prisoner holding up
the broken bottoms of his feet
for the third clubbing as the torturer
gets an erection? Funny stuff.
Then, Latin roots might be like
the foamy blood that emerged
as he said his Hail Marys,
Medivac hovering humorously above
the fires like the *what*,
the angel of death?

You could keep it to yourself,
You could be more or less sophisticated.
You could use something more textural
or something that evokes the scent
evacuating or the stickiness of hennaed
ivory—*something* with *henna*, anyway.
You could wade unceremoniously off
the brink of suburbia, thinking: I could
lay me down my speculations; I could
receive the nest and the axe like any
tree; I could ruminate only physically,
bending with the dusk and without pity,
with darkening resolve and without
hesitation, with affirmation in sorrow
to close the flesh of the carnation
so the seeds may be preserved
in rags in the dura matre and the dirt
properly fecundated forward.

It becomes daybreak with fog
and description, with mistakes
multiplied, the sea itself a mistake
of description, the crab marooned
in the island of the crab, fish images
broken off from exotic accretions
of alluvium—and a man, pants crotch
almost to his knees, Greek fisherman's cap,
mistaking in every direction, but kind
of funny, like a cockroach circumventing
a foot. He makes you want to say funny
over and over till it sounds funny.
He makes you want to do funny things
in public. He makes you want to allow
something to be funny and trust that it is
funny, beyond the mortal and irreligious tomb.

Trouble in Heaven

White carpets are for the dead.
The living walk on pain, as we
know, but the dead, even here,
even the ones who died smiling,
they suffer without rest.
They make me nervous.
I'm so withdrawn in Heaven
I'm like a bus. I fear
I'll never be able to talk
entirely in clichés. I think *lemon*
and someone else's mouth waters.

Sleeping is what you do
when there's nothing else to do,
like now, in heaven. I try to see
if I can fall asleep
with my eyes open. I balance
my body first, then my mind.
I stop smiling and frowning
and I sleep for a moment. Did I
miss anything, a redefinition of self,
one breath of the unconscious double?
I know there were bombs. *Someone*
was tortured for God.

I should shun the devils
as they signal me from the perimeter
flashing a bottle of something
dangerous in the moonlight, calling
me forth, I who grow weaker in heaven,
thinner, translucent, shivering under
blankets? Where is my rag-haired
psychoflower of Purgatory, beating
the pulse in her neck against my mouth
parted in sleep?

I could get involved in a good
science, maybe, and not be caught
dead thinking about God, entertain myself
with six wry anecdotes about metallurgy.
Metallurgy is actually very interesting.
There's a world of color beneath the microscope,
indicating certain things about what acid to use
to accomplish certain things. There's an urgency
with which I make observations for science.
Soon I'll have to burn the holy orchard
to save my life.

There are parts of heaven I like
and will miss: the Godlike vegetables
of my hands, the book from which I rise
to smell a flower, the quiet shelter
of the bed by the moon, the seemingly endless
allotment of time to prepare
a meal and eat it at a table with a proper chair
and a gesture of good will.

I leave them the times tables. I leave them
my white rat, no longer capable of being himself.

MONA LISA SALOY

Missing in 2005: New Orleans Neighborhood Necessities

Mothers and Fathers order the day
Girls may clean clothes
Boys scour steps
Aunts bake and send bread pudding out for tasty replies
Grandmothers guard knee babies
Grandfathers eye the progress of dovetail joints or the pouring of new
pavement
Uncles spin their latest fast steps or two-for-a-nickle tales

Here, history and culture paint our days in an endless fan stroke.
Schooled or street taught, the past sticks to us like sugar on beignets

Mondays, Mothers slow-cook red beans and rice
Fathers bring home hands hardened by knuckle-breaking work and
handshakes
Grandmothers and Grandfathers join weekend suppers and front-porch
rendezvous
Graceful sorrow songs lace the day, or early-morning King Cole moves
to
Afternoon Rhythm and Blues Meters' style, heart-felt hints of love
overcoming hurt
Evening Praise music is hip enough to hear daily
Night-time Ibraham melodies echo lifetimes of urban haunts,
Bullet's Bar, The Parakeet, Winnie's Place, hanging on corners

Boys carry trumpets or tubas and belt tunes on the walk home
Girls or guys sing re-tooled EWF: Earth Wind & Fire, remix they call it,
while waiting for the St. Bernard bus
St. Augustine's Marching 100 practices in Hardin Park after school
Serenading the neighborhood with big band versions of "Earth Wind &
Fire's "Never"
Corpus Christi, Epiphany, or St. Raymond Church Choirs belt Sunday
Ballads
Peopled by parishioners who practice throughout the week
Neighborhood kids grow into choir directors and piano players or
Soloists on Sundays or Saturday vigil Masses
Some sing at Baptist Churches, Beecham Memorial, or 5th African Baptist,
Mt. Zion, African-Methodist-Episcopalian, others where

Saturday nights see them singing and making music in nightclubs across town
Social and Pleasure Clubs parade and hire bands to pour music into every street
Sidewalk audiences blossom and bloom while dancing behind step parades or Second Line Bands.
Such training ground is free flowing, like the humid air,
Heavy with sweat and elbow grease

Parish Islanders

They live in a parish of death
bone tight and white-oyster-shell covered path
boxed cemetery of granite
and stout crosses that can stand the wide sea wind like nothing living.
Flatland water runs with splotches of stars
sandy arroyos where hulls slowly berth in—
sons gone to sea, or further inland to nightless cities.
The land is so wide and low
they huddle the dead in tight graves
and build their houses close like copse coves.
Wind mazes through alleys and backyards.
From wherever you turn you will return to the sea.
What you don't catch through the waves is not brought back with the tide.

The Water

In the morning the water like a deckhand,
a persistent curl against the shore,

who won't back down, take no or be denied.
It is there under the wharf and soon under

the house, whoring with any swamp rat
or snake. It rings cypress knees with pearls—

it dreams under the sun like cut cane,
throwing back the salt you wash away,

then wearing pilings down to air.
Your houses wade on stilts tall as pillars,

their sheet metal skulls bared to a mildewed
sky. Against the fallen trees rain and lapping

tide meet, slapping of nets and fish and
naked children pulling driftwood boats

in one joyful noise around your sleep.
In the afternoon the water is there, only more,

browner and grayer, no sweeping seaweed or foam,
just its presence farther up your shore,

like a dull brother-in-law in front of TV.
He means something to somebody—

but not you, not just now. Its slow wake seems
harmless, the litany of waves before a storm

rolling benignly ashore. Intoxicating!
And then it is there, all gray length of it,

rich sex of it, it wants you so badly,
it pounds at the door, *let me take*

your smallness, your jetties, your broad
coasts, your loam. It gathers

at night beyond the curtain of mosquitoes,
darker than the shut-down sky,

the boarded-up clouds. Its desire
thrums like an idling outboard. Ignore

it and it tows itself into your dreams. It's
everywhere, every chance, all the time.

It is more certain than death or love.
It must have been conceived by death and love.

When the last silt sinks under your feet,
you will have to walk out on this water.

Psalm at High Tide

Rain on the river's vinyl surface:
water that glitters,
water that hardly moves,
its branches witness to trees,
to fronds, leaves, crab floats, pilings,
shopping carts, appliances—
the divine earth takes everything
in its wounded side
and gives back wholeness.
It bears the huddled profane
and endures the soaking
venerated in its wild swirls—
this river fixed with wooden weirs,
radiant in misshapen glory.

The Dirty Side of the Storm

Death just misses you, its well-defined
eye and taut rotation land on
someone else. No need to study the sky

for signs or watch the cows—
not with satellite loops, infrared
imagery, reconnaissance flights shrinking

the orange cones of uncertainty.
If it makes you feel better, go ahead
and push pins through a brittle chart.

Your coordinates square neatly east
of the worst wind shear, lightning
strikes, and bursts of air.

All convection steers clear
of your splattered doorframe.
The Red Cross mobilizes elsewhere.

Take a good look at those oak roots
from a calm doorstep and wait.
The sadness is a surge carrying

all its debris back to you, a flood
that shoves clods of ants and snakes
through your walls and then

sits in your house for days and days.
This is the dirty side of the storm.
Would that Death had blown straight through.

The Curlew

Plate 291 (Numenius borealis)
is the only instance in which the subject
appears dead in the work of John James Audubon.

1.

Beneath the cedars stirring in the churchyard,
stone angels endure the weather for the dead
while townsmen, slinging shovelfuls of dirt,
strive in a singular rhythm. He sits alone
sketching the angels from the shade—*a kind*
of heavenly bird he reasons with himself—
although their wings are broken, faces scarred,
each fragile mouth feigning the same sad smile
as the one before it. Offered double his price
to paint a likeness of the pastor's daughter—
buried for more than a week—he reluctantly
agreed—times being what they are. The men
call from the grave—beckon with their hands
calloused and swollen with the wage of work.

2.

The nervous bird worries the waterline,
probing the sand between the waves' retreat
and surge. Its shrill call dies into a wind
that scours the wide, airy stretch of shore.
How dull it seems against the gulf—with no
raised crest or striking plumage to admire,
no flamboyant breast or ivory bill,
only the markings of a common plover.
And yet he studies it—from behind the dunes—
studies its several postures, grounded and
in sudden flight—and not content to praise
it from a distance, to sacrifice detail,
unpacks his brushes and arranges them
before raising his rifle and taking aim.

3.

The men still beckon from the grave. The angels
seem expectant. In the short walk between the shade
and where they wait, he thinks, for the first time,
of the work ahead. The men, who moments ago
joked about worms and the girl's virginity,
delicately scrape the remaining dirt and clay
off of the coffin's lid. They sweep the lacquer
with their hands. The cedars rattle overhead.
And while they struggle with the lid, he vows
to recreate her—as she might have been—
to excuse her blemishes—whatever they
may be: the sunken features of her face,
her decaying skin—to find the form that once
was there, and, afterward, erase what was.

4.

Wings stiffening against its breast, the curlew
refuses the rigging. Driven by the sun's descent,
a lack of wood, and never being one to work
from memory, he lays it in the sand
beyond the tide's tall reach. Nothing escapes
his hand: from alien feet to modest crown,
the upturned wing and speckled down, the throat,
the meager curve of beak—the small, dark eye.
He thinks it wears its body like a cloak—
or like the white gown draped loosely around
the pastor's daughter, the shadow of the cedars
branching over her folded hands, her chest,
her exposed neck and clavicles—her face
still radiant as if she might sit up to greet him.

The Choice

for the artist

In August, when the drapes seem sheer
against the light of noon and shadows
shrink beneath the wilting blades
of ivy, the gathering birds repeat
their lists of ritual agitations.
Such is their sole inheritance:
a bred desire and fear of silence.

Who can blame the mockingbird
for borrowing the cardinal's song?
I've heard it in the afternoons,
and, unaware, when wandering
alone from room to vacant room,
paused by the phone or in a doorway
and delighted in its music;

and she has surely heard it too,
my neighbor—the widowed curator—
who, haunted by an artist's hunger,
spends her pittance on supplies
and her evenings crouched beneath
a naked bulb to paint again
the likeness of Renoir's *La Loge*.

The heat presses against the panes.
The birds retreat into the leaves.
Perhaps there is no new beauty
in this landscape—only shards
of the forgotten—yet we search
for it, beneath the unexpected
flash of the mockingbird's ascent.

The Seven Thunders

And when the seven thunders spoke, I was about to write;
but I heard a voice from heaven say, "Seal up what the seven
thunders have said and do not write it down."
                        —Revelation 10:4

1.

There is no rain. Not yet.
Only these clouds swelling
with the voice of thunder.

2.

Beneath our fallen leaves,
the copperhead
that scarred my father's hand
uncoils to shed its skin.

3.

I feared that seething hand,
its seven seals coursing
in the blood. Doors shook
in that angry house.

4.

Father of my youth,
why must you reckon
the silence between thunders?

What brace could hold
against the violent winds
gathering in the distance?

5.

When I asked, afraid,
what the thunders were,
he answered, "Our Lord
clapping His hands."

6.

Above the burning dropseed,
the shrike that sings my father's name
spears the snake
on the top strand of barbed wire.

7.

The last peal fades
from the pasture. Rain
pelts the dry clay.

ED SKOOG

Mister Skylight

When you enter the city of riots, confess

what turns your life has taken,
what is hard-on and what is mineral. Confess
until the wind catches itself by the tail.

Or find some solace. Mr. Skylight captains
a houseboat downstream like a vitamin.

I can only just begin to bear the chain-link fence.
Reflected in a puddle, the image trembles
as I tremble. The image freezes, I shiver.

It is like the immensity Gregor Samsa
is hoping to sleep through, but, well, can't.

The woman playing Atari in public has, has. . .
Everything's hauled away. In buckets.

These peaches, for example. I have heard
of you, yes, the monkey says. The moon
offers its offensive and ridiculous bulge.

*

Out in the salvage yard the snowy drifts

are not snow. White paint on frames,
they lean against front doors that won't open in.
Mr. Skylight, stumbling through, asks

"Didn't we just finish painting this wall?"
"Aren't the brushes still drying on the sill?"

When the moment opens again,
remember to feel the immense province
pulling-in, a hand here and here,

remember to smell what first was sweet,
apricots just sliced, one half-globe still rolling.
His wife ran upstairs to call police

as the "assailant took the victim's own
paring knife from the counter."

We show this on the snowy channels
most sets veil, between the black and white:

how they dragged Mr. Skylight inside and made
demands, then went deeper into his building,

and the iron gate lifted off its spindle.

*

Hill of stubble in moonlight, the hog

bristles across the lawn,
eats whole bouquets, eats bouquets whole,
plowing tusk through silk rose, a fresh lily.

Our headstones surrender their salt.
Wilder animals would not perturb us.
Worse hogs will cross and sand

down names. This one, at least, grunts life.
He would eat hog, could he make one die.

If there is a man inside the hog costume,
wanting to feel unchanged, so there is a hog
wearing an interior fake man. How, then,

is the lifeboat going to find us, and will

there be room in a craft so bundled-up
with early survivors, clawing and shouting?

*

When I tell Mr. Skylight my dream

he doubles my prescription. Pen in hand,

he gestures at his shelf of resources
and says *take your pick*. At the same moment,

your butcher jabs his butcher knife
toward the row of basted ham shanks,
take your pick.

We leave the dock at dawn for trout.
What Argonauts we are.

Dawn-lavendered boats bring in night's catch.
I stand above in the gray sweatshirt,
belly full of cauliflower soup,

in a light rain. On the sidewalk, a

teenager repairs a
satellite with a wrench.

*

It is like a hole in an attic
someone has just climbed through.

The river drowns boys who guess wrong.

Eats whole towns. Eats towns whole.
Oak, shark, mansion, whale,

and each mountain that has dared to rise.
I cannot see the words I am thinking.

Looking up, past the water fountain,

I see the Superdome, poached egg
where the Saints play. Some men with ropes
climb the curve, hose whitewash down

Mister Skylight lights a Bulga cigarette
and reclines while the other men work.

Knowing suddenly how, I sing along.
I, too, am tired of miraculous recoveries,

the *mono no aware* of survival,
these supple cancers disappearing

like green jerseys into the skate park.

*

I had forgotten that I had forgotten. I

had one hand in one century's big finish,
a new kind of metal, a bionic art:

it's a story my mother tells, thinking
of the wrong boy. She is old now.
And these stories will be forgotten
umbrellas in the coat check.

Standing on an oil rig looking North
at my country, I watch cigarettes
glow from boats passing in the dark.

On the beach, to make love, the man
and the woman step off the island.

He stares back at land. She, the sky.

A fat fish, days dead, washes up. Crabs
scuttle from the side, pick it clean.

On the exact dune where he fixes his edge,
when he does, a scribbled indecipherment
scrawls vine through the sand. She

navigates by the stars, by Sirius,
the dog. She recognizes her collaborator,

the dizzying recombinations.

*

Windy again on the lakefront last night.

We're getting our own apartment.
Rolled out of bed about one-ten.
Pissed off, I said *I don't think so.*

Sunlight has so little tenure.
He flew out and was hit by a propeller.

The little man, you mean? The boy.
He had fever. I couldn't take him.

But I have always hewed to that music made
from gentle modifications,
the lake-effect modulations

provoked into motion and never
the frame-frozen getaway.

And I said *Donald*. You *can not*
hold him all the time. You got to
put him down sometimes.

*

No one could find the right shoes on sale.

The chancellor ferried the study subjects
and set them loose with steak knives.
After carving up the painting faculty, they began
this serious and important work.

The lights are going down. Your mother stands
at the door, her check for our visit

sweaty in her hand. But I have more to teach.
Listen as I take my paint from this vein
and trace the ocean's dissolve,

dissolve myself and my voice
(at my peril)
                    untie the rendezvous

sleeping city

*

On the garbage truck, the runners hang

half-out, undefined. Shouting they lift

lug, tug, huff, drag, and push
up the bright defecations, Chinese take-out

and new Sonys, the granola salad of litter boxes,
acres of bubble wrap, ripped tissues,

fish gone bad like plague, blood clots,
suppositories, diapers, the vomit
of the cancer patient wiped up with Brawny,

rum vomit of the bright girl,

the sheet music to *Clair de Lune*,
cuttings from a holly, oyster shells
on top, round mirrors of the dawn.

One of the First Questions

when arriving in the desert is how a rented house, some crows,
and sprigs of spring lilac will ever make it into my head, then out
again as language. Never mind, somebody else's bed and mirrors
of moonlight.
                    Even when settled with a cold beer at dusk to count colors
on a paint chart, I am at a loss. Add to that the nightly apparition of my
neighbor who rises before dawn to water and hum to her weeds. Blanket
pulled over my head, I breathe beneath a pillow.
                                        The dog with a rhinestone
collar doesn't change. She falls directly into stanzas. Suzie is always Suzie—
asleep by the mailboxes or chasing cars up the dirt road.
                                                        I walk that road
to the chapel with the big crucifix and outhouse behind it. They've been
here longer than anyone cares to remember. Easter, hooded men still
gather to whip themselves and moan like ghosts. Penitents. Old blood
on their minds, sparkled statue of a horse by somebody's trailer.
Beyond that comes the long view: Plain of tough sage,
Pueblo land all the way past
Sacred Mountain.
                    I write through sun-up and gray days, drag five notebooks,
as if they were the lit ocean floor, for anything resembling my muse.
Fragments
of fragments she can feed me. Leaf shadow from the cool adobe walls.
Imposter,
she whispers, this is not your land.
                            I can't find an opening, or the broom, or even
the hose said to be curled in the rafters. The off button on the alarm clock escapes me
when the neighbor quits watering, and I doze, smothered in covers. But,
let's go back
to my initial question of how to embody another's scented space—all of that
a quandary
until early one Friday
                    I recognize the wind at the screen door, its familiar tap.
Then the clap of pigeon wings, forty of them lifting twenty birds, and by afternoon
burrs thicken my socks after scavenging the plain again. I know those scratches
as I do the cemetery caretaker who only has to glare an off-with-you and slam
his door when he sees me coming. Because of my regular appearances among
the graves, I am rebelliously at home, a squatter of sorts.

Soon the outhouse is mine
too. Wafts of ancient odor spread with grasshoppers in the sage, and the better part
of transmutation comes with restlessness—coyote's howl creeps into my bed
along with the moon. Bark and bay infused with cold blue light. Likewise,
I vibrate with what moves in the desert at night.

The last morning here
an ant crawls diagonally across the page, and three Bosque pears in the painting
want to be jammed in at the end: *Skewed models of balance*, I scribble, then zip
a toy fox in my luggage, lost ancestor of the baby I love well. Also to carry home,
the fresh green wing tattooed on my left ankle—small and solitary,
it marks the way less sure.

Easter Inventory

Easter falls on the first full moon
after the Vernal Equinox so nomadic
pilgrims had enough light to travel by.

Stillness in these moonlit mirrors—
one marked in, the other *deeper*

into wonder.

Hunger and fast fill the blue emptiness
of 4 a.m.   Who am I to question space

in someone else's double bed, sectioned off
for me and god knows what next phantom?

Coyote howls in the high desert. Half asleep,
I mumble, wily move, drawn to the tremors

of another world.

~

Drought again, and magpies fly through in the cottonwoods—
carnival magic on a stick, these raucous birds in black and white.

Two magpies are even hand-painted on the sheet beneath my pillow.

Mythic bird of happiness flattened on pale linen.

Footsteps under the window at night tell me the neighbor's
at it again. Humming, she hoses the wither called her garden.

Maybe a tale is due this dark lady—the one that ends, *And*
as never before, thirty thirsty magpies peck apart the sleepless
creature with its hose of desert water.

~

Sitting in the backyard with paint-charts and cold glass of beer,
I wonder how long a crow can blow about on the branch

and not fly away, while a young Korean lilac roots in arid soil.
Crow flickers in the leaves, the air so dry it glitters, my eyes so

224

parched, they're hard to close. At sunset, I give the birdbath two
cups of water and a chunk of quartz carried home from the canyon

switchback. In town, a nightly drummer calls the hungry for supper.
I won't have this crow to judge when the branch is empty, and I

return to the shades between "ocean cloud" and "deep seashell".

~

If the National Wildlife Fund hadn't sent me the stuffed barn-owl
as a thank-you for my donation, I might not recognize what's calling

in the tree. But I had squeezed that bird each night so my cat could
hear its who-whooos, two short then two long.
                                                    Now an owl filled
with breath echoes at twilight. Vociferous kin, this bird whose fund-raising
twin slept with a cat for months in a house only feet from the Eastern Divide.
You think this an exaggeration? I know how far sound travels.

~

April on the back road to the Penitentes Cemetery where the dusty
lilacs bloom. By evening the stacked mailboxes are empty, and the dog

napping beneath them takes time-out to chase a passing car, or two.
Most slow down, used to Suzie's habits.

Quite a different response from the one nailed up every three feet
to the fence ahead: NO TRESPASSING!!! There's even a huge one

in red propped against the chimney. As I walk by, a boy yells
from the upstairs window, hey lady we own this road, you know.

The holy land he calls it, though in both directions people walk home
with groceries. I grin and bend to pick lilacs through his fence to stick

in Suzie's collar. Photos drop from my folder of the ten-foot black crucifix
this side of Pueblo land and Sacred Mountain. In dream that night, my plane

careens towards chimneys then suddenly floats to a halt above Suzie
asleep in the dirt.

~

Four windows of the chapel are boarded up, and it's hard to find
a door, or to get the story straight about exactly who first crucified
the natives—
                    a long line of penitents ready to flay themselves
for countless Holy Weeks into the future.

Yesterday when asked about the term *arroyo secco*, the cab driver
looked straight at me, and said this was not his people's language,
and drove a whole lot faster.

Behind the chapel there's that black crucifix beside an outhouse
with holes cut in a piece of rotted wood.   Count the years
backwards to when a body finally was nailed up and soldiers
emptied their stomachs under the Easter moon. Humid stench
of relief.

Bright Blessed Days

River wind blows a diesel pall
over the bronze general and horse
in the park. Shuffle here, scuffle there,
a conga line curls around the fountain.
They bang coffee tins marked AIDS.
The voice of Satchmo rises past patio
walls: bright blessed days, dark
sacred nights over outcroppings
of glass that sharpen each locked
garden's secret. Street vendors mix
ripe red strawberries with shouts
of collard greens, a bucket of
scrub-water slopping down
to the chill spring ground.
The cathedral choir sings
to the prayerful, stained glass
brightening another sad family story.
Palm fronds click dice in the breeze. Hope against
hope. What a wonderful world: the crowning wish
scratching its way up and out of Satchmo's earnest throat.

BRIAN SPEARS

Up South

Amy stands on the edge of the sand,
tastes breezes through lips once chapped
by Oklahoma dust, looks away from the neon,
the faux-frontal nudity of Lauderdale.
She is home here, this place of mahi
and yellowfin and shark that flash
through reef and surf, that call her
to rejoin them as though she had once
sprung whole from the sea. Her land,
her peninsula, once separated from
civilization by malarial swamp
that still threatens to reconquer.
She calls my home "up-south."
New Orleans, clichèd home of swooners,
of goateed gamblers debarking
from riverboats, of Storyville quadroons
named by Shakespeare. Not my city.
Mine is patois of immigrants, attendant
in *chère* and *Hey la-bas* and *mais yeah*,
in Ti-Jean and Nookie and Mawmaw June,
in roux dark and sweet and so brown;
in daily August rain not cooling,
falling just enough to steam the streets
and send me running for a nearby bar,
windows painted: *Cold Beer, Colder A/C.*
She is *pollo* and *camaron*, jerk and salsa
and reggae and old Jewish women
mopping their foreheads. I am *bourré*
and *etouffée*, low down papas with
the blues and a city ever on the brink
of washing into the Gulf of Mexico.
She is displaced Irishmen, snugs and whisky,
too many people, ever on the brink
of being blown into the Atlantic.
I am where no one is a stranger,
just misplaced family returned home.
She is where no one is a stranger;
everyone is from somewhere else.

I-55

Swisher Sweets, Heaven Hill Bourbon,
>feet covered in bar grime, driving south
>>at three a.m. Eden is a boat launch

under the Manchac bridge, unspoiled
>for me, anyway. *Turn off the headlights*
>>Eve whispers. Sheriff's office rousts

drunk fishermen and couples like us
>too cheap to hit the No-Tell Motel,
>>and it's not as romantic as it sounds.

Just the last to leave, no one
>to go home to anymore, and tomorrow
>>work starts after dark. No kids until

next weekend, no weed until payday,
>no payday for a week. This is what
>>we have—maybe ten minutes to fumble

with clothes, the splash of startled nutria,
>Avon hand lotion, a three-quarter moon,
>>shoe-crunch on the oyster shell road.

JAMES MARTIN SPEARS

Nudge

Face in hand, Paul Bunyan of a man—
Who's chopped down the chopper? Someone's
broad ax splayed that bark, that hard-wood
resolve to keep straight despite the weather,
bashing back tides of whatever there is for
the universe to toss—how well he would
have ridden North Atlantic swells, but not now;

something now has stricken too deeply,
has nudged the giant a bit off balance,
has forced belated awareness that stiff-spined
oak can't bend much like willow trees;
maybe accretions of indecent people
weigh his boughs, God knows there are
too many of them in far too small a space;

who is he, then—a student, maybe, who's
found that even Ph.D. professors can be as
shallow or more so than the average Joe Blow;
maybe the matter is more meaningful than that,
a man who finds he can't escape himself, and
so he can't hide from despairing over barrages
of thoughts that his sick wife will somehow die;

fearing loneliness, then, maybe is what
assails him, leaned against a buggy full
of nothing at Walmart, leaning on nothing
that is not precarious, that seems sturdy
but yields to the slightest nudge; and so
the man standing by himself with buried
face in hand braces for an impending fall.

SHERYL ST. GERMAIN

Crossing the Atchafalaya

for Greg Guirard

1

our boat cuts through muddy water to black,
water with oxygen to water without
and back again, winding around giant stumps
of old growth cypress, all that's left
from when this swamp was logged to almost
nothing a hundred years ago

if you close your eyes you can imagine them:
thousands upon thousands of living trees
thousands of years old, mute shades
that ghost this almost empty stretch of water

the air would have smelled like cypress then
and the other gone ones—ivory billed woodpeckers—
would have thrived in those thick trunks
that would have risen twenty-five times
taller than us into the heavens

their lime green leaves
would have ceilinged the sky

2

bald cypress lives long
                              but grows slowly

the small trees that dot the Basin now
might be a hundred years old, not yet
mature, though big enough,
some say,

for garden mulch

3

many have disappeared to mulch,
but still there's life here: crawfish burrow
in water around cypress knees, ospreys build nests
on top of dead trees, woodpeckers drum,
barred owls nest in tree cavities,
herons, egrets and Cajuns fish the tea-brown water,
bear and deer, possum and bobcat
fox, coyote and armadillo hunt the edges,
beavers and otter, snakes slither everywhere
there's a giant alligator nearby,
Greg says, but we only look halfheartedly for it

we've seen many over the years
and some things
are better left alone

4

the swamp is hemmed in with levees,
bayous are damned and the river can't move
like it once did, so some days the water goes black
and kills everything caught in it
Greg's crawfish traps are almost empty with the dead today
we boat from trap to trap, *black water* he says
as he pulls up another trap of dead ones

no air in the water
they drowned

5

we know what else lies under these waters:
massive trunks of ancient cypress
                              honey-yellow and auburn,
thick as three alligator bodies, trees felled
from a time when loggers took
everything, and if one fell into the water,
well there was enough to waste

6

just a few of the great giants still stand
in a secret place you can find if you ask

231

we visit them at sundown after the day
of dead crawfish, the waters bloody
from the sinking sun,
                              Spanish moss
glinting silver and hopeful on the limbs of the trees—

the trees that are left: silent and dark guardians
of this rich graveyard, mothers

of the disappeared

            their song haunts me to bone

Addiction

in memory of my brother, Jay St. Germain, 1958-1981

The truth is I loved it,
the whole ritual of it,
the way he would fist up his arm, then
hold it out so trusting and bare,
the vein pushed up all blue and throbbing
and wanting to be pierced,
his opposite hand gripped tight as death
around the upper arm,

the way I would try to enter the vein,
almost parallel to the arm,
push lightly but firmly, not
too deep,
you don't want to go through
the vein, just in,
then pull back until you see
blood, then

hold the needle very still, slowly
shoot him with it.
Like that I would enter him,
slowly, slowly, very still,
don't move,
then he would let the fist out,
loosen his grip on the upper arm—

and oh, the movement of his lips
when he asked that I open my arms.
How careful,
how good he was, sliding
the needle silver and slender
so easily into me, as though
my skin and veins were made for it,
and when he had finished, pulled
it out, I would be coming
in my fingers, hands, my ear lobes
were coming, heart, thighs,
tongue, eyes and brain were coming,
thick and brilliant as the last thin match
against a homeless bitter cold.

I even loved the pin-sized bruises,
I would finger them alone in my room
like marks of passion;
by the time they turned yellow,
my dreams were full of needles.

We both took lovers who loved
this entering and being entered,
but when he brought over the
pale-faced girl so full of needle holes
he had to lay her on her back
like a corpse and stick the needle
over and over in her ankle veins
to find one that wasn't weary
of all that joy, I became sick
with it, but

you know, it still stalks my dreams,
and deaths make no difference:
there is only the body's huge wanting.

When I think of my brother
all spilled out on the floor
I say nothing to anyone.
I know what it's like to want joy
at any cost.

Cajun

I want to take the word back into my body, back
from the northern restaurants with their neon signs
announcing it like a whore. I want it to be private again,
I want to sink back into the swamps that are nothing
like these clean restaurants, the swamps
with their mud and jaws and eyes that float
below the surface, the mud and jaws and eyes
of food or death. I want to see my father's father's
hands again, scarred with a life of netting and trapping,
thick gunk of bayou under his fingernails,
staining his cuticles, I want to remember the pride he took
gutting and cleaning what he caught; his were nothing
like the soft hands and clipped fingernails that serve us
in these restaurants cemented in land, the restaurants nothing
like the houses we lived and died in, anchored in water,
trembling with every wind and flood.

And what my father's mother knew:
how to make alligator tail sweet, how to cut up
muscled squirrel or rabbit, or wild duck,
cook it till it was tender, spice it and mix it all up
with rice that soaked up the spice and the game so that
it all filled your mouth, thick and sticky, tasting
like blood and cayenne. And when I see the signs
on the restaurants, *Cajun food served here*,
it's like a fish knife ripping my belly, and when I see
them all eating the white meat of fat chickens
and market cuts of steak or fish someone else
has caught cooked cajun style, I feel it
again, the word's been stolen, like me,
gutted.

DAVID STARKEY

The Age of Sponges

Precursors of bathtub sponges were
the dominant species on the planet
for as long as 100 million years.
    —*Nature* magazine

It was an epoch unmarked by significant
development in the arts and sciences.

            Indeed, the chief glory of the era
was its changelessness, the flow and ebb
                    of food entering pleated body
walls, then being sluiced back out to sea

        by a tidal surge that served as a kind
of Julian calendar. No intellect or rage

                marred the salty universe. Instinct alone
mattered, an organism's ability
                        to regenerate. The sorry state
at which they would eventually arrive—

        as cleaning implements, contraceptives
and cartoons—remained in some inconceivably

                complex future. The moon arose, then gave
way to the sun. The vast waters plunged
                        ashore, retreated. Thousands of hundreds
of millions of days passed in a nerveless,

        bloodless state of bliss, or what passes
for bliss among those who cannot name it.

Blues for Deborah Digges

Now, the swish of your hair is unlike
a eucalyptus tree in afternoon wind,

your eyes are not remotely akin
to fish scales shimmering in sunlight.

Nothing about you resembles an unsigned
guestbook collecting dust

in the alcove of an unvisited
museum, or a series of weathered

handbills pasted to the side
of a condemned building.

No, when you leapt from the upper
level of the U Mass football stadium,

you left behind language and all
its derivatives: your nine brothers

and sisters, your prodigal son,
and your three husbands, the last

of whom preceded you, as the obituaries
have it, in death. Jesus, but you

could write—hard- and wild-eyed
in the same damned line—so it must

have hurt like hell to pause
on that precipice, abandoning

your singular gift, knowing not a single
syllable would catch you when you fell.

JENNIFER STRANGE

Improvisation: Lullaby

Frantic jazz tonight—
a manic cymbal
falls every third beat

in my bedside radio.
My father played
the same station

at the household hour
when he, half-sitting,
had the one light on.

We came to listen:
scales at the harsh seventh
he stretched his neck to—

singing, as if he knew
every syncopation
while mom fixed her face.

Then he turned off the light,
talked low and strained at her
like string bass to clarinet, dissonant.

Here Grows Her Face

Monkeyflowers lining our road chose oddly well:
after all this rain, they might as well be streamside.
They catch the water our vines let go,
brick red bells leaning on their pickets.

This is spring in my hometown, early though it pours.
It holds back the mosquitoes until my mother turns fifty
(twice my age, twice her age when she birthed me).
She drove her young hands early from bush to bush:

azalea, clumsy wisteria, lazy rosemary, lone dogwood,
and that surprise iris embracing her chain link fence.
We freed it and her Cocker Spaniel ate it proudly—
they whither in a day or less. Let the flicker and the robin

sing to her, or at least to the grass grown long
and the cars thick with pollen, all the wipers seriously wiping
the windshields fogged from humidity and bodies so cold.
I will take her hand to walk among it when she at once grows old.

On the Death of a Mouse

A mouse is made that small for speed, not smarts,
so when one tries to cross a busy road,
it meets (perhaps) a car. Not quite dead then,
spasming up from asphalt like a bag
caught sideways in the wind, a mouse requires
some mercy, some swift end. And I might think
how easy, how abrupt that sentence seems.
This is my right on earth, and duty too,

for beauty flees this place like coastal rains:
complete, completely fast. It takes a year
or two to see the vapors pass, or else
a moment. We too, like some mouse, do writhe
and spasm all our days until at last
we come to what we've earned, that death so late
for all we've run across. And mercy may
make much of me, as only mercy can.

Pulling Cotton

Long rows planted late in spring
in a feast of bottomlands cleared
for crops when we were young,
cotton grew flawless next to our
house, painting all the fields new
colors once a year. Shared acres
chopped by hand with filed hoes
blossomed red and pink by end
of summer, then broke like heat
into grown bolls for fall-bearing
harvest. Children of means, we
knelt in those fields among rows
of white wealth, pulling cotton
two hands at a time longer than
the light lasted. Paid two cents
a pound cash, scales in the field,
we felt as free as we ever would,
filling handed down canvas sacks
with a full day's labor that weighed
on our shoulders like prayer.

The Pool Hall

Lucky to find a place to stand, we'd watch
the money players shoot ten-cent snooker
for dollar bills, their handwork on the cue
a lost art, chalk on the tips a blue sign
of their intent. Never masters of the game,
we could always tell when someone made
a good shot. The room would become still
just long enough to nod praise and hear
the sounds of old men whistling the past.
Driving through seventeen years later,
I stop to look, but the pool hall's gone,
a dollar store in its place and no sounds
of snooker anywhere. Someone had run
the tables. On the way to an older south,
I fill the tank and take the long road out,
leaving behind too soon the discount
signs of a new place we once called home.

The Hunter

Nine years old and never fired a shot to kill
before today, his first aim
hit a yellow breasted robin perched
halfway up a gum tree fronting the porch
of his own house. Shooting a barrel-rusted
BB gun borrowed for the day,
he felt the worn stock begin to peel
against his skin. Without sound, the little
ball of steel barely flicked a feather,
entering the breast clean as a piston,
the way he imagined it could.
Waiting in place to see the shot take,
he watched the robin fall, landing
on the sidewalk like a plastic sack of sugar
tied together with red string.
Putting the gun down beside the dead game,
he went looking for someone to tell,
the truth of his aim too much to hide.
Soft and flat, the bird's fall made a sound
he can still hear sometimes, seeing again
that shade-tree morning years ago
when his perfect prey, too small to mount
and no good to eat, turned stiff,
before he could pick it up and walk away.

L.E. SULLIVAN

The Loved Woman

I want her to climb inside my skin so
when we walk hand in hand
along red speckled railroad tracks,
beneath full magnolia trees,
with alabaster blooms
curving like her hips,
she can be warm in me
when we arrive to find the quarter
dressed in glowing candles.

She'll stay
and only go
where we go together
in the early morning
wide open, but
full of stamen stalks,
as night falls
full of love and loss

Cows on High

for Clare Potter

Cefn-Onn Ridge above Cardiff, Wales:
In a hill meadow near moss-covered
ruins of Castell Morgraig, we found
cow places pressed in wild grass.
Sheep played there, too, remember?—
leaving behind their clues,
little tufts of white wool
snagged on heather, blackthorn.
We took turns sinking into cow imprints
wishing the peace of slow,
brown-eyed beasts would flow into us.

Vermillion Parish, Louisiana:
Clare, there's a photo of a lone
white house on a small hill,
like a grandma's house, pecan pie and coffee.
The home is an island,
pasture replaced with storm surge from the salty gulf.
Hurricane Rita.
Cows that sought high ground,
maybe a hundred cows, look at you,
peer from every window,
stand jammed on steps and porch,
pushing ponderous heads through
balusters, breaking them.

TOM WHALEN

Tomato

Once, like all things, it was a single line, a tongue
down the spine, but now it makes a cloud, a surround
and a sound red as rain. It does in fact rain here,
from within and without, and within again.
A pulpy moon that fell to earth, was pulled
by the tides or, perhaps, a memory of tides,
which is what tides are. If it lacked wisdom
it would have been a stone, but wisdom we know
rains. And all this wetness is of the ocean.
No seed soaks so long; thus the fruit
could hardly be other than it is. Sweetly drunk,
like a monk, I encounter its perfection even
in my dreams. Not the rock-like apple, but this:
the embodiment of tautness. What else opens
the sky, lavishes the sun with such drippings?
It wants to fall, not orbit. If you wait long enough
with outstretched hand, it will come to you.
Such power in complacency! A mansion of suns,
or at least a rooming house where all the inhabitants
want to escape. A pressure outward, like the universe.
Perhaps, finally, a universe that will never collapse,
no matter whether drawn or quartered. It's skin
(the outer layer of the universe) a tension film
that, once broken into finite galaxies, star clusters,
will reseed the ether, reform space.
On this round table I've stacked several as high
as I can. When they fall, they do not bruise
like children or bananas. An adult object, then,
yet somehow (in song?) brother to the frog.
Birds search here for their liquid young.
Parenthood as perfection, but equally
something wishing to be held, handled,
laid in laps. Light gathers in its crevices.
Nowhere, not even when split open,
does darkness obtain. Light, as a liquid,
is not yellow; rain, as light,
is red—what surrounds the surround.
And, again, the sound a red song,
and a ripeness, which is what death is.

Getting Back to Him

It takes longer than I remember,
like the train that went in circles
around a mountain I'd never seen,
and at the top was one of those old
medieval castles you see when travelling
up the Rhein. It's like a toy
you forgot in the rain and one day
you see it in some other kid's yard,
and you think it's yours, but
you're no longer sure. It could
belong to the kid with the missing finger
swinging in the low branches of a tallow tree.
And besides, you don't even know
if you want it, it's broken, its back
is cracked, its color gone. It's like
that, or something like that, trying
to get back to him, and you don't even know
why you try. He never held out his hand
with a ripe plum in it. He never wrapped
you up like a loaf of bread overnight.
When you clapped your hands or called,
he didn't come like a good dog. Instead,
he spun like a top. That was his game.
Spinning. You couldn't control him. You
couldn't walk away. He was with you
in his spinning, sucked you up
like you were flotsam in a whirlpool.
And now you want to get back to him.
What madness. What nonsense for the
birds to feast on, if there were any,
but there's only a little memory,
perhaps, something left over from dream
you can't quite dredge up, a glimmer,
tinfoil in the grass, light sluicing
all over the yard, and the boy spinning.

Simple Sonnet

A simple sonnet need not follow the rules
to the letter. Take rhythm, for example, which Cecil
Taylor once described as "the space of time
danced thru." The poem can adjust its iambic robes
and as quickly take off its hat of rhyme, leaving
the meat of the matter, its internal form to figure.
Which is easier said than done, as we all know,
except in a simple sonnet where the argument
may be the image of a boy for the first time
on the high board, sheets of light crinkling below,
while the other kids shout and taunt him to dive
("You chicken or what? Do a somersault, a back flip")
and the board is a line and each step a word
and the end springs the boy into the blue above.

GAIL WHITE

On the Death by Drowning
of My Favorite New Orleans Restaurant

The corner of Canal and Carrolton
sheltered Mandina's, where for seventeen
years every Saturday they poured me one
black Russian followed by trout amandine
or the best shrimp loaf on the whole Gulf Coast.
But now the watermark is at my eyes,
the floors have rotted, and the stolid ghost
of a decayed refrigerator lies
prone on the sidewalk. And I'm shedding tears
over a stack of dishes, one of which
I'll steal in memory of those seventeen years
that made their gumbo and my life so rich.
Come back, my love! Serve me on shining dishes
my weekly miracle of loaves and fishes.

Azalea Street Winter

On bad days, the loony lady across the street
holds her wine by the neck and tells us all
that the question of her identity
has fuck to do with neighborhood,
and that the big blue Impala with the wire wheels
better slow the fuck down. The Impala stops
at her knees and spins its engine, threatening
to break itself apart. And a white-haired baby
cries beyond them on the asphalt lot.

On good days it's the trees you notice,
and no one minds the radio. Cool winds
carry dust out the window. Crazy Hoot
only laughs on her front step, whistles at the postman,
who tells me she's all right. At night, under the orange light,
under the live oaks, under my window
a girl with high brittle hair sits on the bench
and watches her white-haired baby play. He falls,
laughs, runs, falls again.

ANDY YOUNG

Woman Dancing on Her Son's Coffin, New Orleans, 1995

from a black and white photograph
at the House of Dance and Feathers

She is not
      in black not
        weeping, not leaning
against someone as she staggers,
            drunk with grief, no—

She dances on top
          of her son's coffin
          outside the Lafitte Projects
      where he was gunned down.
She dances and dances
             unbending, limbs thrashing
        like Kali
            on Shiva's ashen body.

Gray clothes—
          are they sweats?—
sway in the sun-blasted noon,
          her two living boys
        make music around her:
D-Boy gone
      who that killed D-Boy who
first told her the news? She can't,
      some funneled shape
          his horn won't blow.

No lace,
      no shawl across her shoulders.
Bare-armed, back cocked,
          ass out, she dances, yes—

—another thud of percussion—

I, no   she
          grunts,
             pushing him out
ripping open at Charity,

                    fluorescent lights
                    backlighting his arched shape

          —bright slash of the trumpet—

he burns with fever,
                    laughs at ice
          tracing
          the pouting lips

                    late July, night blooming jasmine
                         thick in the mouth

                    I grab another sliver
                         —slap of snare—

—no, she does,
                         it's her boy,

a number now
          pushing up the murder graph
                    like a thermometer

                         oh mama mama

          Men hauling the casket bend
at the knees
                    not from weight
                         but from bass thump,
from tuba's
          fat momentum.

          Her sweats shift
soft and loose
          as they play it loose and mean,
                    a threat in the throb
the trombone moans
                    she's gone

past shiver
          past flash of brass glint
                    & casket shine underneath her feet

          she shakes her head—look:
                    she's turning to look
                         into everyone's face.

                              249

Altars for the Murdered Dead

New Orleans, 2008

1.

Wreaths, seven-day candles piled on a step:
a woman stabbed behind the door boarded
with plywood. The shiny yellow crime ribbon
stripes her shotgun house like ribbons on tree
trunks up North where I read her mother waits.
When firemen hacked down her door to find her,
we'd driven past the Cop-Lab trucks
and my friend said *must be someone's dead,*
like that, like *wonder when the rain will stop,*
our daughters in the backseat chirping words.

2.

I bring a bunch of flowers for Ahmed,
head shaved, thick ridge of staples
across his skull like train tracks, arms
strapped down with plastic manacles.
I don't know him, his brain shifted
so far in his skull all the wires scrambled.
His eyes slide back as if his mind swims
home to Alexandria's fishing boats.

3.

At the gas station, I watch on closed circuit
the silent film repeat on its split screen
the various angles of his beating,
watch again and again the truck
approach from the hotel behind.
I want to rewind the reel, edit out
his head cracking against the counter,
but he lies there as his brain swells,
flickers in side view, wide angle,
panoramic vision. He lies there
in black and white, and in the real
greens and metal of his room.

4.

A stuffed bear's stuck in a shutter, and all
the plants she had in the house hang outside
in wilting light. She studied pollination,
the paper says, worked at the plant shop
by the U-Haul where we bought our dewdrop tree.
Someone's nailed a letter to her door,
notebook paper in a plastic sheath
to protect it from the elements. *Dear Jess,*
it starts, but I don't read anymore.

Voyeur

*It's like being shot from a potato gun—no
a pineapple cannon* my neighbor says of death,
of his heart stopped and started
three times to get it back in sync.
He lifts his shirt to show me,
through the iron fence, electric burns
from the paddles, skin raised in the shape
of clumsy oven mitts on his chest and back.

Early forties, he's young for this, and lucky;
his heart sack had heaved wrong
for a long, long time.
Later, in his dormer window,
two forms—his and some
new girlfriend's?—make
acrobatic love, angling and pressing,
sections of flesh flattening against glass.

I am dumb before it, remembering
all the years of his Pearl Lounge
parties, famous for their decadence,
even in New Orleans, his stripper wife
naked on the bar, slathering molasses
on her skin as she danced, and he,
mixing drinks, tossing bits of down
into the air so that they landed on her

and stuck, the rest of the night spent
tarred and feathered. Back then,
he didn't know. But shouldn't he be
tamer now, having woken one day to find
he should be dead? It is a little sad to know
the bar—a jumble of old ironworks
and junk: a huge, mechanical ostrich,
a pillar that holds nothing up—is quiet. . .

not because I'll miss the people inside
who sizzled all night, frayed and reeling,
but because the party had to stop
because death was found inside it,
rank as a bloated cat found
under a porch. The bodies are still
at it, against the beveled glass. That window
could open, send them tumbling down

to lumber and shards. A tumor could sprout
in some unwidowed room of her body,
he could wake one day craving the taste
of gunmetal. Look: the lights behind them
silhouette their shapes. The scrawny
moon devours itself over everything.
Lovers, turn out those lights. Lie there
in the dark and listen to each other breathe.

THE POETS

RALPH ADAMO began to teach English at Xavier University in fall of 2007 and to edit the *Xavier Review* in the spring of 2011. His six collections of poetry were all published by small presses, most recently the selected volume *Waterblind* from Portals Press in 2002; he won a National Endowment for the Arts award for poetry in 2003. Former editor of *New Orleans Review* and *Barataria Review*, Adamo has taught at most Louisiana area universities and continues to work as a journalist. In the months following Katrina, he was awarded a Katrina Media Grant by the Open Society Institute to pursue the story of the radical changes being wrought in local public education. Among his other books are two from Lost Roads Publishers, *Sadness at the Private University* (1977) and *The End of the World* (1979), and one from New Orleans Poetry Journal Press, *Hanoi Rose* (1989).

EMILY ALLEN graduated from the Louisiana School for Math, Science and the Arts before attending Hendrix College in Arkansas. She holds a Masters in Southern Literature from the University of Arkansas and is currently a Ph.D. candidate in poetry at the University of North Texas. A teaching fellow, as well as an adjunct instructor at Mountain View Community College in Dallas, Allen is interested in the teaching of writing at all levels. She has previously been published in the *Xavier Review*.

Having recently completed the requirements for an M.F.A. in Creative Writing and an M.A. in English at McNeese State University in Lake Charles, Louisiana, LOU AMYX studied playwriting under the mentorship of Lanford Wilson during three semesters in the Edward Albee New Playwrights Workshop while completing a B.A. in Creative Writing at the University of Houston. Her poems appear in *The Naugatuck River Review*, *The Arena*, and the forthcoming *Multi-Culti Mixterations* anthology. Amyx is a founding member of Yellow Flag Press, an independent publisher of limited edition poetry broadsides.

BARRY JEAN ANCELET is Granger & Debaillon Endowed Professor of Francophone Studies and Folklore at the University of Louisiana at Lafayette. He has published articles and several books on various aspects of Louisiana's Cajun and Creole cultures and languages. He is involved in the production of festivals (including Lafayette's Festivals Acadiens et Créoles, which he directs), special concerts, records, museum exhibitions, documentary films, and television and radio programs (such as the "Rendez-vous des Cadiens," a weekly live radio show from the Liberty Theater in Eunice, Louisiana). Normally, he has written poetry in French under the pseudonym

Jean Arceneaux. His recent English efforts were inspired by his daughter Clélie and his wife Caroline, both poets themselves.

CAROLINE ANCELET is a wife, the mother of five children, and a teacher at Acadiana High School near Lafayette. In the summer of 1994, she became a fellow with the Acadiana Writing Project, which opened a new world of expression for her. Though she rarely has time to write for pleasure, once a year she joins her Acadiana Writing Project fellows deep in the piney woods at Camp Hardtner, where she spends two days writing with Darrell Bourque. The poems included here all come from those experiences. Like most of her writing, they are about negotiating the tricky waters of relationships.

JOHN ANDERSON is a native Louisianan who moved away many years ago. His love of poetry, folklore, and fiddling eventually brought him back home, where he received his M.F.A. in poetry from McNeese State University. He then entered the University of Louisiana at Lafayette's Ph.D. program and is currently an English candidate, concentrating in linguistics. He's been published in *The Southern Review* and is also an assistant editor for *Rougarou*, an online journal sponsored by the University of Louisiana.

RANDY BATES' publications and credits include a book of nonfiction, *Rings: On the Life and Family of a Southern Fighter* (Farrar, Straus & Giroux); work in *Grand Street*, *Ploughshares*, and *New Orleans Review*; and a writing fellowship from the National Endowment for the Arts. He teaches at the University of New Orleans.

JACK B. BEDELL is the Woman's Hospital Distinguished Professor in the Humanities at Southeastern Louisiana University where he also serves as editor of *Louisiana Literature* and director of Louisiana Literature Press. His most recent books are *Call and Response* (Texas Review Press), *Come Rain, Come Shine* (Texas Review Press) and *French Connections: A Gathering of Franco-American Poets* (LaLit Press).

STEVE BEISNER is a Louisana native who divides his time between New Orleans and Santa Barbara, while writing poetry, short stories, and long fiction. He's currently working on a collection of New Orleans Bar poetry and a novel set in South Louisiana. Beisner is co-editor of *Ink Byte* online magazine for writers.

GLENN J. BERGERON II is a funeral director and embalmer in Thibodaux, Louisiana, where he lives with his wife, Samantha, and son, Aodhan. When not undertaking the preparation and burial of the dead, he operates Chicory Bloom Press, an independent press that publishes poetry chapbooks. His own work has appeared in *Louisiana Literature*, *The Louisiana English Journal*, and *Hellas*.

JOHN BIGUENET is the author of *The Torturer's Apprentice: Stories* and *Oyster*, a novel, among other books, as well as such award-winning plays as *The Vulgar Soul*, *Rising Water*, and *Shotgun*. His poetry, stories, and essays have appeared in such magazines as *Esquire*, *Granta*, *North American Review*, *Playboy*, *Southern Review*, *Storie* (Rome), *Story*, and *Zoetrope* as well as in various anthologies, including *Contemporary Poetry in America* and *Uncommonplace: An Anthology of Contemporary Louisiana Poets*. He has twice been elected president of the American Literary Translators Association. An O. Henry Award winner for his short fiction and a New York Times guest columnist, he was poet in residence at the University of Arkansas at Little Rock and at the University of Texas at Dallas. Currently, he is the Robert Hunter Distinguished University Professor at Loyola University in New Orleans.

JOHN BLAIR graduated with a Ph.D. from Tulane University in 1989 and was born in St. Petersburg, Florida. His poetry collection, *The Green Girls*, was the 2003 winner of the Lena-Miles Wever Todd Award from Pleiades Press, and his short story collection, *American Standard*, was the 2002 winner of the Drue Heinz Literature Prize and was published by the University of Pittsburgh Press. He has poems and stories in *Poetry*, *New York Quarterly*, *Sewanee Review*, *Antioch Review*, *New Letters*, and elsewhere. He is on the faculty at Texas State University, where he teaches American Literature and directs the undergraduate creative writing program.

BEAU BOUDREAUX recently won the New Dawn Unlimited Chapbook Competition for his manuscript, *Significant Other*. His poems have recently appeared in *Antioch Review*, *Cream City Review*, *Louisiana Literature*, and *Margie*. He teaches English in Continuing Studies at Tulane University in New Orleans.

LOUIS BOURGEOIS is the Executive Director of VOX PRESS, INC, a non-profit avant-garde literary press. His most recent book publications include *Hosanna*, a collection of aphorisms released in the summer of 2010 by Xenos Books, and *The Animal*, published by BlazeVOX. His translations of Rimbaud's major prose poems are due for release by Xenos Books in 2011. Currently, Bourgeois lives, edits, and writes in Oxford, Mississippi, where he is accompanied by two daughters and his wife, the artist and singer-song writer, Betsy Chapman.

DARRELL BOURQUE is Professor Emeritus in English from University of Louisiana at Lafayette and served as Louisiana Poet Laureate, 2007-08 and 2009-11. His poetry books are *Plainsongs* (Cross-Cultural Communications, 1994); *The Doors between Us* (Louisiana Literature Press, 1997); *Burnt Water Suite* (Wings Press, 1999); *The Blue Boat* (The Center for Louisiana Studies Press, 2004); *Call and Response, Conversations in Verse* (with Jack B. Bedell, Texas Review Press, 2009); *In Ordinary Light: New and Selected Poems* (University of Louisiana at Lafayette Press, 2010); and *Holding the Notes* (a special commissioned chapbook, Chicory Bloom Press, 2011).

ANN REISFELD BOUTTÉ, who grew up in New Orleans, writes essays, feature stories, and poetry. Her work has appeared in many publications. She has a Master's Degree in Journalism from American University and has worked as a feature writer for a daily newspaper and a national wire service. In 2009, she won third place in the Artists Embassy International's Dancing Poetry Contest and an honorable mention in the Texas Poetry Calendar awards. She was a Juried Poet in the Houston Poetry Fest in 2001, 2005, and 2009.

ALLEN BRADEN, the author of *A Wreath of Down and Drops of Blood* from University of Georgia Press, has received fellowships from the NEA and Artist Trust as well as the Emerging Writers Prize, the Grolier Poetry Prize, the Dana Award in Poetry and other honors. After earning M.A. and M.F.A. degrees at McNeese State University, he returned to Washington State.

CATHARINE SAVAGE BROSMAN, who lives in Houston, is Professor Emerita of French at Tulane University. In addition to scholarly books, she has published two volumes of creative prose, seven collections of poems, and four chapbooks. Her recent collections, *Range of Light* (LSU Press, 2007) and *Breakwater* (Mercer University Press, 2009), received starred reviews in Booklist. In 2011, LSU Press will bring out another collection, *Under the Pergola*, and Mercer will publish *On the North Slope* in 2012. Her poems have appeared in *Sewanee Review*, *Southern Review*, *Critical Quarterly*, *South Carolina Review*, *American Scholar*, *Southwest Review*, and *First Things*. French translations of her poems have been published in the *Nouvelle Revue Française*, *Europe*, and elsewhere.

STEVEN C. BROWN, JR. and the photographer, Jerry Uelsmann, recently collaborated on a book entitled, *Moth and Bonelight* (2010), published by 21st Editions, in which Brown's poems were paired with Uelsmann's imagery. Brown's poem, "Penumbra," appears in *Best New Poets 2010*, selected by Claudia Emerson. Previous and forthcoming publications include *Barrow Street, Asheville Poetry Review, Indiana Review, Measure, Rattle*, and *Unsplendid*. Brown is currently a Ph.D. student in Harvard's History of American Civilization program.

ELIZABETH BURK is a psychologist who currently divides her time between a private practice in New York and a husband in southwest Louisiana. Her work appears or is forthcoming in *Atlanta Review, Rattle, Louisiana Review, South Carolina Review, Wisconsin Review, Red Wheelbarrow, Spillway, Workers Write! Tales from the Couch Edition*, and other journals. She is presently on leave from a low residency M.F.A. program at Spalding University in Kentucky.

KELLY CHERRY has published twenty books of fiction, poetry, and nonfiction, eight chapbooks, and translations of two classical plays. Her most recent titles are *The Woman Who*, a collection of short stories (2010), *The Retreats of Thought: Poems* (2009) and *Girl in a Library: On Women Writers & the Writing Life* (2009). Her short fiction has been reprinted in prize anthologies and she received the Dictionary of Literary Biography Award for the best volume of short stories published in 1999. Other awards include the Hanes Poetry Prize for a body of work in that form, a USIS Speaker Award, and fellowships from the Rockefeller Foundation and NEA. In 2010 she was a Director's Visitor at the Institute for Advanced Study in Princeton. She is Eudora Welty Professor Emerita of English and Evjue-Bascom Professor Emerita in the Humanities at the University of Wisconsin-Madison. She and her husband live in Virginia.

WILLIAM BEDFORD CLARK is professor of English at Texas A&M University, where he has taught since 1977. He has published widely on various topics in American literary study and is General Editor of the Robert Penn Warren Correspondence Project. His poems have appeared in a range of little magazines and leading quarterlies.

CARLOS COLÓN is the author of twelve chapbooks, including *Mountain Climbing* and *Clocking Out*, two collections of haiku and concrete poetry; *Sassy*, a collection of linked poems written with Alexis Rotella, and *Circling Bats, Wall Street Park*, and *Autumn Leaves*, three books of concrete renku written with Raffael de Gruttola. His work has appeared in numerous publications, including *Modern Haiku, Journal of Poetry Therapy, Writer's Digest*, and *Louisiana Literature*. His poetry has also been part of three public art projects. In addition, Colón edited *Voices and Echoes*, the 2001 Haiku Society of America Members' Anthology and is editor of Shreve Memorial Library's Electronic Poetry Network (http://www.shreve-lib.org/poemofday.htm). His most recent chapbook, *The Inside Scoop: New and Selected Poems*, was published by Naissance in 2010.

PETER COOLEY is Professor of English and Director of Creative Writing at Tulane. He has a B.A. in Humanities from Shimer College, an M.A. in Art and Literature from The University of Chicago, and a Ph.D. in Modern Letters from The University of Iowa, where he was a student in the Writers' Workshop. His eight books of poetry are *The Company of Strangers, The Room Where Summer Ends, Nightseasons, The Van Gogh Notebook, The Astonished Hours, Sacred Conversations, A Place Made of Starlight*. Carnegie Mellon, his publisher, released his new volume *Divine Margins* in 2009. Cooley's poems have appeared in such magazines as *The New Yorker, The Atlantic, Poetry, The*

Nation, The New Republic and in over one hundred anthologies. From 1970-2000 he was Poetry Editor of *North American Review*.

SIDNEY MCCALLUM CREAGHAN was born very close to the banks of the Mississippi River in Baton Rouge, Louisiana. She now resides in Lafayette, Louisiana, where she has a practice in Jungian oriented counseling. Creaghan is a visual artist and maintains a studio at Rue du Pont Gallerie in Breaux Bridge, Louisiana. Her poetry and her paintings have won awards. Creaghan is still married to her first husband and together they are enjoying the blessing of their first grandchild.

KEVIN CUTRER was raised in Kentwood, Louisiana. He has published poems in the *Hudson Review*, *The Dark Horse*, *Texas Review*, *Louisiana Literature*, *Raintown Review*, *Unsplendid* and elsewhere.

KATE DANIELS was educated at the University of Virginia (B.A. and M.A. in English Literature) and Columbia University (M.F.A. School of the Arts). Her teaching career has taken her to the University of Virginia; the University of Massachusetts at Amherst; Louisiana State University; Wake Forest University; Bennington College; and Vanderbilt University, where she is associate professor of English and Chair of the Vanderbilt Visiting Writers Series. Her first book of poetry, *The White Wave* (Pittsburgh, 1984), won the Agnes Lynch Starrett Poetry Prize. Her second volume, *The Niobe Poems* (Pittsburgh, 1988), received honorable mention for the Paterson Poetry Prize. *Four Testimonies*, her third volume, was one of Dave Smith's selections for his Southern Messenger Series, published by LSU Press (1998). A fourth volume, *A Walk in Victoria's Secret*, will appear later this year in the same series. She was recently named the winner of the 2011 Hanes Award for Poetry by the Fellowship of Southern Writers for her work to date.

JOHN DOUCET is Distinguished Service Professor of Biological Sciences and Director of the University Honors Program at Nicholls State University. He is a genetics researcher and educator, specializing in genetic diseases in Louisiana families. He is also the author of fourteen plays, all based on Louisiana history and culture, and has been awarded the Louisiana Native Voices and Visions Playwriting Award and the Louisiana Division of the Arts Fellowship in Playwriting. He is author of two books of poetry, *A Local Habitation and a Name: Poems from the Lafourche Country*, and the forthcoming *Where Sea Creates the Past*. In addition to scientific papers, plays, and poetry, Doucet has written and edited historical nonfiction, including *The Cheniere Caminada Story*, *Lafourche Country II*, and the recently released *Lafourche Country III*.

LENNY EMMANUEL, internationally published poet and essayist, became Contributing and Managing Editor of *The New Laurel Review* in 1998. He is also editor of *HEARTHS*. *The Icecream Lady*, his first collection of poems and essays, was published in 1997 by Ramparts, Inc. and Indiana University; his second collection, *Blue Rain*, is forthcoming in November, 2010. His *Elements of Prose* is published by Ramparts. Recent poems have appeared in *Parnassus*, *Free Lunch*, *SLANT*, *Pegasus Review*, *Plainsongs*, and *Agenda* (the British issue of American Poets). Having degrees in chemistry, business, and English, he held dual appointments in pathology and English for twenty-seven years at Indiana's University Medical Center in Indianapolis. From Savannah and Tybee Island, Georgia, he currently lives in Pass Christian, Mississippi.

JAMES ENELOW is nearing the age of responsibility. He has found a nice house, the love of a good woman, and a girl who thinks of him as the "World's Best Daddy."

His love and skill in poetry was nurtured under Stephen Gardner and honed in the land of Louisiana and Texas.

GINA FERRARA works as an educator and lives in New Orleans. She received her M.F.A. in Creative Writing from the University of New Orleans. Her chapbook, *The Size of Sparrows*, was published by Finishing Line Press. Her poems have appeared in numerous journals including *Poetry East*, *The Poetry Ireland Review*, and *Callaloo*. She currently coordinates Poetry Buffet, the monthly reading series sponsored by the New Orleans Public Library. Her latest collection of poems, *Ethereal Avalanche*, was published by Trembling Pillow Press in the fall of 2009.

ANNE MARIE FOWLER is currently a doctoral student at The Union Institute & University where she is completing her dissertation. She holds a Master of Fine Arts from Spalding University. Her creative work has appeared in several national and international literary journals, and the anthology *Coloring Book: An Eclectic Anthology of Fiction & Poetry by Multicultural Writers* (Rattlecat Press, 2003). She has published academically in several encyclopedias and currently teaches composition, literature, creative writing, research writing, and mythology at the undergraduate and graduate levels.

A native and long-time resident of Mississippi, JOHN FREEMAN now lives in Harvey, Louisiana, where he is a retired teacher. His poetry has appeared in *Arkansas Review*, *Hawaii Pacific Review*, *The MacGuffin*, *Roanoke Review*, and *Xavier Review*. He has published three books of poetry, the most recent *In the Place of Singing* (Louisiana Literature Press, 2005). He taught English and creative writing at Tarleton State University and Mississippi State University. He is currently poetry editor of *The Magnolia Quarterly*.

JOHN GERY's books of poetry include *Charlemagne: A Song of Gestures* (1983), *The Enemies of Leisure* (1995), *American Ghost: Selected Poems* (English-Serbian, trans. by Biljana Obradovic, 1999), *Davenport's Version* (2003), *A Gallery of Ghosts* (2008), and *Lure* (English-Serbian, 2010). Other books include *Nuclear Annihilation and Contemporary American Poetry: Ways of Nothingness* (1996), (with others) *In Venice and in the Veneto with Ezra Pound* (2007), and (with Vahe Baladouni) *Hmayeak Shems: A Poet of Pure Spirit* (2010). Gery's work has appeared in journals throughout the U.S. and Europe, and he has done collaborative translations from Armenian, Chinese, French, Italian, and Serbian. A recipient of fellowships from the NEA, Louisiana Division of the Arts, Institute for Advanced Study, University of Minnesota, and Fulbright Foundation, he is Research Professor of English at the University of New Orleans and directs the Ezra Pound Center for Literature, Brunnenburg, Italy. A Louisiana resident since 1979, he lives in New Orleans with his wife, poet Biljana Obradovic, and their son Petar.

JESSE GRAVES was born and raised in Sharps Chapel, Tennessee, forty miles north of Knoxville, where his family settled in the 1780s. He is an Assistant Professor of English at East Tennessee State University, where he joined the faculty in 2009 to teach classes in creative writing and American literature. He received a Ph.D. in English from the University of Tennessee and a Master of Fine Arts in Poetry from Cornell University, and has taught at the University of Tennessee, Cornell, and the University of New Orleans. Graves's poems have appeared in recent issues of *Appalachian Heritage*, *Connecticut Review*, and *Tar River Poetry*.

Born and raised in New Orleans, CHRIS HANNAN is a graduate of the College of the Holy Cross in Worcester, Massachusetts, where he received a B.A. in the

Classics. His poetry has appeared in *Magnolia Quarterly*, *The Purple*, *Desire Street* and *The Classical Outlook*. He was awarded First Prize in the 2004 Gulf Coast Writers' Association's annual Let's Write contest for his poem "Pointing to the Brain." Most recently, his poem "Epithalamion" was selected as a runner-up in the Poetry Division of the 2010 Faulkner-Wisdom Creative Writing Competition, sponsored by the Pirate's Alley Faulkner Society and judged by poet Nicole Cooley. The poem will be published in a special online edition of the Society's publication *The Double Dealer*. Hannan recently graduated from the Loyola University, New Orleans, College of Law, and is currently an attorney in the New Orleans offices of Baker, Donelson, Bearman, Caldwell and Berkowitz. He and his wife Emily live in New Orleans.

Published in the United States, Canada, and Malaysia, RABIUL HASAN's work has appeared in more than forty journals and anthologies, such as *Mississippi Writers: Reflections of Childhood and Youth*, *The Rockford Review*, *Writers' Forum*, *The Macguffin*, *Poet Lore*, *Permafrost*, and *Louisiana English Journal*. He is the author of one collection of poems entitled *Madonna of the Rain*, published in 2008 by Rockford Writers' Guild Press in Rockford, Illinois. In addition, he has a critical book entitled *Rediscovering Hemingway in Bangladesh and India, 1971-2006*, to be published this fall by University Press of America, Inc. Hasan, who earned a Ph.D. in English (American Literature) at Texas Tech University, is assistant professor of English at Southern University in Baton Rouge, Louisiana.

ASHLEY MACE HAVIRD's chapbook, *Dirt Eaters*, was published by the South Carolina Poetry Initiative in 2009. Her poems have appeared in many journals, including *Southern Review*, *Shenandoah*, *Southern Poetry Review*, *Tar River Review*, *Texas Review*, *Calyx*, and *Southern Humanities Review*. Her short stories have appeared in *The Virginia Quarterly Review* and elsewhere. In 2002 she was awarded a Louisiana Division of the Arts Fellowship in Literature and was nominated for inclusion in the Pushcart Prize Anthology. In 2000 and in 2007, she received the Shreveport Regional Arts Council Fellowship in Literature. She has taught Creative Writing at Centenary College of Louisiana, the University of Virginia's Division of Continuing Education, and the Renzi Education and Art Center in Shreveport, Louisiana.

DAVID HAVIRD grew up in Columbia, South Carolina, and attended the University of South Carolina, where he studied under James Dickey. He earned his doctorate at the University of Virginia and since 1988 has taught English at Centenary College of Louisiana. His publications include poems and articles on such Southern writers as Dickey, Flannery O'Connor, Elizabeth Spencer, and Allen Tate, in *Agni*, *The New Yorker*, *Poetry*, *Sewanee Review*, *Shenandoah*, *Southwest Review*, *Texas Review*, *Virginia Quarterly Review*, *Yale Review*, and elsewhere. His collection, *Penelope's Design: Fourteen Poems*, won the 2009 Robert Phillips Poetry Chapbook Prize (Texas Review Press, 2010).

AVA LEAVELL HAYMON is a poet, playwright, and teacher. Her poems have appeared in the journals *Poetry*, *Southern Review*, *Prairie Schooner*, *The Sun*, and many others; in five chapbooks from independent small presses; and in three collections, *The Strict Economy of Fire*, *Kitchen Heat*, and *Why the House Is Made of Gingerbread*, from Louisiana State University Press. She won the *Louisiana Literature* Prize for poetry in 2003, and the L. E. Phillabaum Prize for 2010. She teaches poetry writing in Baton Rouge, Louisiana, during the academic year and in New Mexico in the summer, where she directs a retreat center for writers and artists. She has directed workshops and read her poems widely, in the United States and in Canada.

Louisiana native DIXON HEARNE teaches and writes in southern California. His work has been twice nominated for the Pushcart Prize, and his new book, *Plantatia: High-toned and Lowdown Stories of the South*, is nominated for the 2010 PEN/Hemingway award and recently won the 2010 Creative Spirit Award-Platinum for best fiction book. Other work appears in *Louisiana Literature, The Louisiana Review, Post Road Magazine, Cream City Review, Wisconsin Review, Roanoke Review, The MacGuffin*, and many other magazines and journals. He was a featured speaker at the 2009 Louisiana Book Festival and is currently at work on new poetry and short story collections.

JACK HEFLIN's second collection of poetry *Local Hope* was published in 2010 by the University of Louisiana at Lafayette Press. *The Map of Leaving* (Arrow Graphics, 1984) won the Montana First Book Award. His poems have also appeared in many journals, including *The Antioch Review, Poetry Northwest, Nimrod, Willow Springs, Missouri Review, Green Mountains Review* and *Poetry East*, and in several anthologies, such as Sarabande books' *A Fine Excess: Contemporary Literature at Play*. He has been awarded Writing Fellowships from the Missouri Arts Council, the Montana Arts Council, and the Louisiana Division of the Arts. In 2008 the Louisiana Endowment for the Humanities awarded him an Individual Achievement in the Humanities. He is an Endowed Professor of English at the University of Louisiana at Monroe where he co-directs the Creative Writing Program and coedits *turnrow: A Journal of Fine Arts* and turnrow books.

CAROLYN HEMBREE has poems published or forthcoming in *American Letters & Commentary, Colorado Review, Indiana Review, Jubilat, New Orleans Review, Poetry Daily*, and *The Yale Anthology of Younger American Poetry*, among other journals and anthologies. Her poetry manuscript was a finalist for the following contests: Marsh Hawk, Omnidawn, Poets Out Loud, and Zone 3. It was a semi-finalist for Cleveland State University's First Book Competition. Her poetry has received three Pushcart Prize nominations and a Louisiana Division of the Arts Fellowship Award in Literature. Before receiving her M.F.A. from the University of Arizona, she found employment as a cashier, housecleaner, cosmetics consultant, telecommunicator, actor, receptionist, paralegal, coder, and freelance writer. Hembree lives in New Orleans.

Over the years, JESSICA HENRICKSEN's work has appeared in many journals, such as *Willow Springs, New Orleans Review, The Hollins Critic, Nebraska Review, Bitter Oleander*, and *Cincinnati Review*. Henricksen has twice been nominated for a Pushcart Prize and was the recipient of a grant from the Louisiana Division of the Arts. Most recently, she is the winner of the Ellipsis Poetry Prize. Henricksen is a native New Orleanian. She received her B.A. from Loyola University and an M.F.A. in Creative Writing from Eastern Washington University.

JULIA JOHNSON's poems have appeared in such journals as *Third Coast, Poetry International, Cake Train*, and *Greensboro Review*. Her first book of poems, *Naming the Afternoon*, was published by the Louisiana State University Press in 2002. She was the winner of the Fellowship of Southern Writers' New Writing Award. Johnson is a native of New Orleans.

ALLEN C. JONES was born in Northern California, but his mother was raised in New Orleans on Annunciation Street. Curious about the South and this side of his family, Allen came here to pursue a Ph.D. at University of Louisiana Lafayette in English. His work has appeared in *Rougarou: An Online Litererary Journal, Flaming Arrows* (Ireland), *The Bitter Oleander*, and *The GSU Review*.

A native of Boston, JULIE KANE has lived in Louisiana for more than three decades. Her two most recent poetry collections are *Rhythm & Booze* (2003), a National Poetry Series winner and finalist for the Poets' Prize, and *Jazz Funeral* (2009), which won the Donald Justice Poetry Prize. Her poems have been featured on *Poetry Daily, Verse Daily,* and *The Writer's Almanac,* as well as in journals such as *Southern Review, Antioch Review, Prairie Schooner, Louisiana Literature,* and *Feminist Studies.* She is an associate editor of the Pearson/Longman Southern literature anthology *Voices of the American South* (2005) and the co-editor, with Grace Bauer, of *Umpteen Ways of Looking at a Possum: Critical and Creative Responses to Everette Maddox* (2006). A former George Bennett Fellow in Writing at Phillips Exeter Academy, New Orleans Writer in Residence at Tulane University, and Fulbright Scholar to Vilnius Pedagogical University (Lithuania), she teaches at Northwestern State University in Natchitoches, Louisiana.

RICHARD KATROVAS is the author of seven books of poetry (three published by Wesleyan University Press, four by Carnegie Mellon University Press), a novel, a collection of stories and two memoirs. He taught for twenty years at the University of New Orleans and presently teaches in the Ph.D. and M.F.A. programs at Western Michigan University. He is the founding director of the Prague Summer Program, which is going into its seventeenth year. Katrovas's poems, stories and essays have appeared in many leading journals and anthologies, and he has been the recipient of numerous grants and awards.

DAVID KIRBY is the author or co-author of twenty-nine books, including the poetry collections *The House on Boulevard St.: New and Selected Poems, The Ha-Ha, The House of Blue Light,* and *The Travelling Library,* in addition to the essay collection *UltraTalk: Johnny Cash, The Mafia, Shakespeare, Drum Music, St. Teresa Of Avila, and 17 Other Colossal Topics Of Conversation.* His many awards include the Guy Owen Prize, the James Dickey Prize, the Brittingham Prize, and fellowships from the National Endowment of the Arts and the Guggenheim Foundation. Kirby's *Little Richard: The Birth of Rock 'n' Roll* (Continuum, 2009), has been hailed by the *Times Literary Supplement of London* as a "hymn of praise to the emancipatory power of nonsense." Kirby's latest book of poetry is *Talking About Movies With Jesus,* and he is the Robert O. Lawton Distinguished Professor of English at Florida State University, where he has taught since 1969. See also www.davidkirby.com.

JOHN CANTEY KNIGHT, a Georgian, now lives in Louisiana. He has published poems extensively for the past twenty years. He is the recipient of a number of awards, including the *Louisiana Literature* Award for Poetry, the Langston Hughes Poetry Prize (Tom Dent Literary Festival), and the Pirate's Alley William Faulkner Award for Poetry. In 2009, *Body into Earth,* his first book of poetry, was published.

YUSEF KOMUNYAKAA was born in Bogalusa, Louisiana, in 1947. His numerous books of poems include *Pleasure Dome: New & Collected Poems, 1975-1999* (Wesleyan University Press, 2001); *Talking Dirty to the Gods* (2000); *Thieves of Paradise* (1998), which was a finalist for the National Book Critics Circle Award; *Neon Vernacular: New & Selected Poems 1977-1989* (1994), for which he received the Pulitzer Prize and the Kingsley Tufts Poetry Award; *Magic City* (1992); *Dien Cai Dau* (1988), which won *The Dark Room Poetry Prize; I Apologize for the Eyes in My Head* (1986), winner of the San Francisco Poetry Center Award; and *Copacetic* (1984).

BILL LAVENDER moved to New Orleans from Arkansas in 1975 and has been there ever since. He is now the director of the Low Residency Creative Writing program at the University of New Orleans and Managing Editor of UNO Press.

Lavender's books include *Memory Wing* (Black Widow Press, 2011, forthcoming); *Transfixion* (Trembling Pillow and Garret County Presses, 2009); *I of the Storm* (Trembling Pillow, 2006); *While Sleeping* (Chax Press, 2004); *look the universe is dreaming* (Potes and Poets, 2002); and Guest Chain (Lavender Ink, 1999). He also edited the anthology, *Another South: Experimental Writing in the South*, from University of Alabama Press (2003). His poetry and essays have appeared in numerous print magazines including *Praire Schooner*, *Jubilat*, *New Orleans Review*, *Gulf Coast*, *Skanky Possum*, *YAWP*, and *Fell Swoop*, and web publications including *Exquisite Corpse*, *E•ratio*, *CanWeHaveOurBallBack*, and *Nolafugees*. He has published scholarship in *Poetics Today* and *Contemporary Literature*.

KEAGAN LEJEUNE's poems have appeared in recent issues of *Xavier Review*, *Louisiana Literature*, *Texas Review*, and *Borderlands*. LeJeune was born in Louisiana and currently lives in Lake Charles. LeJeune teaches folklore and undergraduate creative writing at McNeese State University.

LAURA MATTINGLY came to Louisiana via a homemade raft down the Missouri and Mississippi rivers from Kansas City, Missouri, approximately 1,500 river miles, and arrived in New Orleans the day after Thanksgiving, 2007. She grew up in San Clemente, CA, and received a B.A. in Literature and Creative Writing from University of CA, Santa Cruz in 2006. Mattingly has been writing poetry since age seven, and she has been organizing community poetry events since 2001. Her poetry has been published in the *Big Bridge New Orleans* poetry anthology and in *Maple Leaf Rag*.

MARTHA MCFERREN received a B.S. and M.L.S. from North Texas State University (now the University of North Texas) and an M.F.A. from Warren Wilson College. She is the author of four books of poetry: *Delusions of a Popular Mind* (New Orleans Poetry Journal Press), *Get Me Out of Here!* (Wampeter Press), *Contours for Ritual* (LSU Press) and *Women in Cars* (Helicon Nine Editions). Her poems have appeared in *Georgia Review*, *Shenandoah*, *Poetry*, *Southern Review* and many other periodicals. She has been awarded an Artist Fellowship in Literature by the Louisiana State Arts Council, a Yaddo Fellowship, and a National Endowment for the Arts creative writing fellowship. She lives in New Orleans with her husband, Dennis Wall.

MICHAEL P. MCMANUS' awards in poetry include a Fellowship from the Louisiana Division of the Arts, The Virginia Award from *The Lyric*, and The Ocean's Prize from *Sulphur River Literary Review*. His poems appear in *Soundings East*, *Texas Review*, *Rattle*, *Louisiana Literature*, *Prism International*, *Atlanta Review*, and *Burnside Review*, among others.

KEVIN MEAUX was born in Kaplan, Louisiana, and educated at the University of Louisiana at Lafayette. His writing has received numerous awards, including a Ruth Lilly Fellowship as well as a Louisiana Division of the Arts Artist Fellowship. His poems have appeared in such journals as *Southern Review*, *Poetry*, *Prairie Schooner*, and *Shenandoah*.

ROBERT MENUET is the founder and first publisher of *Desire Street*, the publication of the New Orleans Poetry Forum. He has published in *The New Orleans Review*, *The Magnolia Review*, and *Desire Street*, and he has led workshops in writing and performance at the Arts Council of Baton Rouge, Barnes and Noble, and in New Orleans. Menuet has performed his poems at The Baton Rouge Gallery, The Baton Rouge Poetry Slam, and in Natchez, Houston, and in New Orleans venues such as The Neutral Ground, The Gold Mine, Sweet Lorraine's, The Dragon's Den, and Le Petit Théâtre du Vieux Carré.

DAVID MIDDLETON is Poet-in-Residence at Nicholls State University in Thibodaux, Louisiana. His books of poetry include *The Burning Fields* (LSU Press, 1991), *As Far as Light Remains* (The Cummington Press, 1993), *Beyond the Chandeleurs* (LSU Press, 1999), and *The Habitual Peacefulness of Gruchy: Poems After Pictures by Jean-Francois Millet* (LSU Press, 2005). Middleton has also published several chapbooks of poetry, the latest of which is *The Language of the Heart* (Louisiana Literature Press, 2003). In 2006 Middleton won The Allen Tate Award for best verse published in *Sewanee Review* for 2005. In November 2006 Middleton won the State of Louisiana Governor's Award for Outstanding Professional Artist for 2006 (for his poetry). Middleton's verse has appeared in *Southern Review, Sewanee Review, Louisiana Literature*, and elsewhere.

JEN J. MOODY was born in New Iberia and raised in Texas. She's currently a graduate student in Creative Writing at Eastern Washington University. Returning to Louisiana sometime in the future is high on her list of priorities.

GEOFF MUNSTERMAN is a poet from Plaquemines Parish and a NOCCA graduate whose work appears in *YAWP, The American Journal of Poetry, Poets for Living Waters, Spillway Review, The Levee Review, Culture Sandwich*, and *Storysouth* among others. He was awarded the Pirates' Alley Faulkner-Wisdom Prize and Overture Awards as well as the John Crowe Ransom Prize in 2006.

KAY MURPHY received distinction for her M.F.A. thesis from Goddard College in 1980. It was published in book form as *The Autopsy* by Spoon River Poetry Press in 1985; her second collection, *Belief Blues*, was released in 1999. Since coming to the University of New Orleans in the fall of 1984, she has published over fifty reviews and essay reviews of contemporary poetry in national journals such as *The American Book Review* and *The Spoon River Poetry Review*. Among the poets she has published work on are: Louise Glück, W.D. Snodgrass, John Haines, Martha Collins, Allison Joseph, and Carl Phillips. Her latest review is on the critic Camille Paglia's *Break, Blow, Burn*. Besides reviews, Murphy has published fiction in such journals as *Ascent* and *Fiction International*. Her poetry has appeared in *Seneca Review, College English, North American Review, Poetry*, and *Chelsea*. She is poetry editor of *Bayou*.

STELLA NESANOVICH, retired Professor of English from McNeese State University in Lake Charles, Louisiana, is the author of *A Brightness That Made My Soul Tremble: Poems on the Life of Hildegard of Bingen* (Blue Heron Press, 1996) and *Vespers at Mount Angel: Poems* (Xavier Review Press, 2004) and editor of *Points of Gold: Poems for Leo Luke Marcello* (Xavier Review Press, 2005). Her poetry has appeared in several anthologies, including *Uncommonplace: An Anthology of Contemporary Louisiana Poets* (LSU Press, 1998) and *Hurricane Blues: Poems About Katrina and Rita* (Southeast Missouri State University, 2006), and in numerous journals and magazines, including *The Christian Century, Christianity and Literature, Modern Age, Chronicles, Xavier Review, Poet Lore, America, The Anglican Theological Review*, and elsewhere. She has fiction in *Southern Review* as well as *Something in Common: Contemporary Louisiana Stories* (LSU Press, 1990). In 1999 she received an artist fellowship from the Louisiana Division of the Arts. She was nominated for a Pushcart Prize in 2009.

JAMES NOLAN's latest book, *Perpetual Care*, was awarded the 2009 Next-Generation Indie Book Award for Best Short Story Collection, and his novel *Higher Ground* won the 2008 William Faulkner-Wisdom Gold Medal. His collections of poetry are *Why I Live in the Forest* and *What Moves Is Not the Wind*, both from Wesleyan University Press. A regular contributor to *Boulevard*, his writing has appeared in *Southern Review, Georgia Review, Poetry, Shenandoah, Utne*, the anthologies *New Orleans Noir* and *The*

Gastronomica Reader, and the *Washington Post*, among other places. He has translated Pablo Neruda's *Stones of the Sky* (Copper Canyon Press) and *Longing: Selected Poems of Jaime Gil de Biedma* (City Lights Books), and is the author of *Poet-Chief* (University of New Mexico Press), a study of Whitman and Neruda. The recipient of NEA and Fulbright fellowships, he has taught at universities in San Francisco, Florida, Barcelona, Madrid, and Beijing, as well as at Tulane and Loyola in New Orleans. A fifth-generation native of the Crescent City, he lives in the French Quarter.

TANIA NYMAN was born and raised in New Orleans, Louisiana. She earned an M.F.A. from George Mason University. Her work has appeared in UNO's *Ellipsis* and in an edition of Robert Atwan's *America Now*. Currently she teaches at Louisiana State University and lives in Baton Rouge.

BILJANA D. OBRADOVIC, poet, translator, Professor of English and Creative Writing (Poetry) at Xavier University of Louisiana in New Orleans, has published two collections of poems: *Le Riche Monde* and *Frozen Embraces*. A third, *Little Disruptions*, is forthcoming. Her work is also in *Three Poets in New Orleans*. She has translated (from and to Serbian) collections of poems by John Gery, Stanley Kunitz, Patrizia de Rachewiltz, Niyi Osundare, Bruce Weigl, Bratislav Milanovic, and Desanka Maksimovic. She has also edited and translated an anthology called *Fives* of Serbian and American poets. Her poems recently appeared in such anthologies as *Like Thunder: Poets Respond in Violence in America* and *Key West: A Collection*.

SUE OWEN taught as the Poet-in-Residence at Louisiana State University and received the Professional Artist of the Year Award from the Louisiana State Arts Council. She is the author of four books of poetry: *Nursery Rhymes for the Dead* (Ithaca House, 1980), *The Book of Winter* (Ohio State University Press / *The Journal* Award, 1988), *My Doomsday Sampler* (LSU Press, 1999), and *The Devil's Cookbook* (LSU Press, 2007). Her poems have been published in national magazines and anthologies, including *Harvard Magazine, Iowa Review, Louisiana Literature, Massachusetts Review, The Nation, New Orleans Review, North American Review, Ploughshares, Poetry*, and *Southern Review*, as well as *The Best of Intro, The Poetry Anthology: 1912-2002, Uncommonplace: An Anthology of Contemporary Louisiana Poets, The Yellow Shoe Poets: 1964-1999*, and *USA Poetry*. After living in Baton Rouge for thirty years, she and her husband retired from LSU and now live in Cambridge, Massachusetts.

MELINDA PALACIO divides her time between Santa Barbara and New Orleans. Her chapbook, *Folsom Lockdown*, won Kulupi Press' Sense of Place 2009 competition. Her poems have been published in diverse journals and anthologies including *Maple Leaf Rag III and IV: An Anthology of New Orleans Poets, Poets of the American West: An Anthology of Eleven Western States, San Pedro River Review, Buffalo Carp, Naugatuck River Review, Black Renaissance Noire*, and *Palabra: A Magazine of Chicano & Latino Literary Art*. Her novel, *Ocotillo Dreams*, was recently published by ASU Bilingual Press.

MICHELE POULOS's poems and fiction have appeared in *Crab Orchard Review, Copper Nickel, Sycamore Review, storySouth*, and other journals. Her book reviews appear in *Blackbird*. She was a finalist for the 2008 Charles Johnson Student Fiction Award. She is a two-time nominee for inclusion in the anthology *Best New American Voices* (Harvest Books, 2008 and 2009). She is pursuing her M.F.A. in poetry at Arizona State University.

WYATT PRUNTY is the author of *The Times Between* (1982), *What Women Know, What Men Believe* (1986), *Balance as Belief* (1989), *The Run of the House* (1993),

Since the Noon Mail Stopped (1997), *Unarmed and Dangerous* (2000), and *The Lover's Guide to Trapping* (2009), published by the Johns Hopkins University Press. His critical works are *"Fallen from the Symboled World": Precedents for the New Formalism* (Oxford University Press, 1990) and *Rationed Compassion: Poetry since World War II*, forthcoming. He has received Guggenheim, Rockefeller, Johns Hopkins, and Brown Foundation fellowships, and is a member of the Fellowship of Southern Writers. Editor of *Sewanee Writers on Writing* (Louisiana State University Press, 2000), he served as general editor of the Sewanee Writers' Series and directs the Tennessee Williams Fellowship program at Sewanee, where he founded and directs the Sewanee Writers' Conference.

JULIA RAMSEY is a New Orleans native recently returned from a too-long stint in New England. She enjoys the poetry of Howard Nemerov and Elizabeth Bishop and is the co-founder and co-editor of *Interrobang?! Magazine* (http://interrobangzine. com). She is the recipient of the 2009 and 2010 Nancy Potter Academy of American Poets award from the University of Rhode Island.

MARTHE REED has published two books, *Tender Box, A Wunderkammer* (Lavender Ink) and *Gaze* (Black Radish Books), as well as two chapbooks, *(em)bodied bliss* and *zaum alliterations*, both part of the Dusie Kollektiv Series. Her poetry has appeared in *New American Writing, Golden Handcuffs Review, New Orleans Review, HOW2, MiPoesias*, and *Exquisite Corpse*, among others, and is forthcoming from *Ekleksographia* and *Fairy Tale Review*. Her manuscript, *an earth of sweetness dances in the vein*, was a finalist in Ahsahta Press' 2006 Sawtooth Poetry Contest. She edits Nous-zot Press, http://nous-zot.blogspot.com/ and directs the Creative Writing Program at the University of Louisiana, Lafayette.

RACHEL REISCHLING grew up in a small town in central Louisiana. She attended Centenary College of Louisiana, where she earned her B.A. in English and Music; afterwards, she graduated from The Ohio State University with a Master of Fine Arts in Poetry. She entered the workforce briefly as a reporter for a small newspaper in southern Louisiana. Most recently, she is earning her Masters of Music at Northwestern State University in Natchitoches. Her poems have appeared in *Quiddity International Journal* and in *Flint Hills Review*.

BRAD RICHARD's book *Motion Studies*, winner of the 2010 Washington Prize, will be published in 2011 by The Word Works. He is also the author of the collection *Habitations* (Portals Press, 2000) and the limited edition chapbook *The Men in the Dark* (Lowlands Press, 2004). His poems and reviews have appeared in *American Letters & Commentary, Bayou, Guernica, Hunger Mountain Review, The Iowa Review, The Laurel Review, Literary Imagination, Prairie Schooner, The Massachusetts Review, Mississippi Review, New Orleans Review, Passages North*, and other journals. Recipient of fellowships from the Surdna Foundation and the Louisiana Division of the Arts, and 2002 poetry winner in the Poets & Writers, Inc., Writers Exchange competition, he is chair of the creative writing program at Lusher Charter School in New Orleans.

Athough best known for his songwriting, ZACHARY RICHARD has published three volumes of French language poetry: *Voyage de nuit* (originally published in 1986 and re-edited in 2001, Les Intouchables, Montréal), *Faire Récolte* (Les Editions Perce Neige, 1997), awarded the Prix Littéraire Champlain in September 1998 by the Conseil de la Vie Française en Amérique, and *Feu* (Les Intouchables, Montréal, 2001), which received the Prix Roland Gasparic in Bucharest, Romania. Richard's contributions to the arts and to French culture were recognized by the government of France in 1997 when he was decorated Officier de l'Ordre des Arts et Lettres in a ceremony at the Quai d'Orsay in Paris. That same year, Richard was initiated into the Ordre des Francophones d'Amérique, in Québec. He is a member of the Ordre de la Pléiade and and honorary member of the Order of Canada (2010). He has received honorary doctorates from the University of Louisiana at Lafayette, the University of Moncton (New Brunswick), and l'Université de Sainte-Anne (Nova Scotia).

GEORGE F. RIESS is a graduate of Tulane University with majors in music and English literature. He is also a graduate of Louisiana State University Law School, a practicing attorney in New Orleans, Louisiana, and a law professor in trial advocacy at Tulane University Law School. His poetry has been published in numerous online and print publications, including *The Pioneer, Louisiana Review,* and *The Magnolia Quarterly.* He was awarded the First Place Prize in Poetry in the annual writing contest sponsored by the Gulf Coast Writer's Association in May, 2010 in its publication, *The Magnolia Review.*

DENISE M. ROGERS received the M.F.A. from the University of Arkansas-Fayetteville and currently teaches composition, literature, and humanities courses at the University of Louisiana-Lafayette. Her poems have appeared in *Louisiana Literature, Alaska Quarterly Review, Borderlands: Texas Poetry Review, Ekphrasis, Mid-America Poetry Review,* and *Xavier Review,* among others. In 2000, she was the recipient of an Artist's Fellowship from the Louisiana Division of the Arts. In 2004, her poem "Snow Falling on Small Town" won the Louisiana Literature Poetry Prize. Her first book, *The Scholar's Daughter,* was published by Louisiana Literature Press in 2008.

A native of Worcester, Massachusetts, DAVID ROWE lives in the Treme neighborhood of New Orleans. His poetry has appeared in such literary magazines as *North American Review, Cortland Review, Big Bridge, Exquisite Corpse,* and *Dorado.* He's been featured on the internet radio program *The Moe Green Poetry Hour* and has served as poet-in-residence at the Beauty Shop, New Orleans. His full-length collection, *Unsolicited Poems,* is forthcoming this summer from Verna Press. His website is www.myspace.com/davidiotraw.

Since 1990 WILLIAM RYAN has co-directed the M.A. in creative writing at The University of Louisiana at Monroe, where he has held both the Tommy and Mary Barham Endowed Professorship in English and the Endowed Professor of English Chair. He co-edits the literary journal *turnow* and ULM Press. His novel, *Dr. Excitement's Elixir of Longevity,* was published in New York by Donald I. Fine, Inc. and was reprinted in paperback with the Laurel Trade Paper division of Dell Publishing. Lynx House Press published two books of his poetry, *Eating the Heart of the Enemy* and *To Die in Latin.* The New Jersey Council on the Arts twice endowed him with writing fellowships, and in 1994 he received an Artist's Fellowship from the Louisiana Division of the Arts. Ryan has the M.F.A. degree from the University of Massachusetts-Amherst and the M.A. from Colorado State University.

MONA LISA SALOY's collection of verse, *Red Beans and Ricely Yours: Poems,* won the PEN/Oakland Josephine Miles Prize in 2006 and the T. S. Eliot Prize in Poetry for 2005, published by Truman State University Press; also, this collection was finalist for the Morgan Prize from Story-Line Press. In October of 2006, The National Constitution Center in Philadelphia commissioned Saloy to compose and perform a poem entitled "We," celebrating 2006 Liberty Medal Recipients: President William J. Clinton and President George H.W. Bush. Saloy's Ph.D.in English was earned from Louisiana State University in Baton Rouge where she also received the M.F.A. in Creative Writing. Saloy earned the M.A. from San Francisco State University and the B.A. from the University of Washington, Seattle.

JEAN-MARK SENS lives in Thibodaux, Louisiana where he is Collection Development Librarian at Nicholls State University and teaches culinary classes at the Chef John Folse Culinary Institute as adjunct Chef. Born in France and educated in Paris, Sens has lived and taught in the American South for over fifteen years. He earned a MLIS from U.S.C. and holds degrees in English from the University of Southern Mississippi and Paris VII University, as well as an Associate in Science in Culinary Arts from Johnson & Wales. Red Hen Press in California published his first collection, *Appetite*, in the fall of 2004.

MARTHA SERPAS's two collections of poetry are *Côte Blanche* (New Issues, 2002) and *The Dirty Side of the Storm* (Norton, 2007). Her work has appeared in *The New Yorker*, *The Nation*, and *Southwest Review*, and in anthologies such as *Bearing the Mystery: Twenty Years of Image*, *The Art of the Sonnet*, and the *Library of America's American Religious Poems*. A native of Bayou Lafourche in south Louisiana, she is involved in efforts to restore Louisiana's wetlands. She teaches creative writing at the University of Houston and is a hospital trauma chaplain.

MICHAEL SHEWMAKER received his M.F.A. from McNeese State University and was recently named a finalist for the 2009 Morton Marr Poetry Prize. His poems appear or are forthcoming in *Atlanta Review*, *Tar River Poetry*, and *Asheville Poetry Review*, among other journals.

ED SKOOG is the author of *Mister Skylight* (Copper Canyon Press, 2009) and *The Swordfish Bicycles* (Copper Canyon Press, forthcoming). He lived in New Orleans from 1998-2005, working at the New Orleans Museum of Art, New Orleans Center for Creative Arts, and Tulane University.

The Swing Girl, KATHERINE SONIAT's fifth collection of poems, is forthcoming from Louisiana State University Press in 2011, and *A Raft, A Boat, A Bridge*, forthcoming from Dream Horse Press in 2012. *The Fire Setters* is available through the Web del Sol/Literary Reviews Online Chapbook Series. Earlier collections include *A Shared Life*, winner of The Iowa Poetry Prize and a Virginia Prize for Poetry. New work is in recent issues of *Iowa Review*, *Denver Quarterly*, *Antioch Review*, *Hotel Amerika*, *Mid-Amercian Review*, *American Poetry Journal*, and *IMAGE: Art, Mystery, Faith*. She teaches in the Great Smokies Writing Program at UNC-Asheville.

BRIAN SPEARS lived on the north shore of Lake Pontchartrain (or thereabouts) between the ages of 7 and 30. He still misses Louisiana terribly. He is the poetry editor of *The Rumpus* (www.therumpus.net); his first collection of poems, *A Witness in Exile*, was recently published by Louisiana Literature Press. His poems have appeared in *Quarterly West*, *The Southern Review*, *storySouth*, *Measure*, *Louisiana Literature* and elsewhere. Brian was a Stegner Fellow at Stanford University from 2003-2005 and currently teaches creative writing and literature at Florida Atlantic University.

After getting out of the Army in 1996, JAMES MARTIN SPEARS moved to Lake Charles to marry his wife, a Louisiana native. They have been married for thirteen years. Spears spent more than half of those years attending McNeese State University where he earned a Bachelor of General Studies, a Bachelor of Arts in Sociology, and a Master of Arts in English. He is now an instructor of English composition at Louisiana State University at Eunice.

A native of New Orleans, SHERYL ST. GERMAIN has taught creative writing at The University of Texas at Dallas, The University of Louisiana at Lafayette, Knox College and Iowa State University. She currently directs the M.F.A. program in

Creative Writing at Chatham University where she also teaches poetry and creative nonfiction. Her work has received several awards, including two NEA Fellowships, an NEH Fellowship, the Dobie-Paisano Fellowship, the Ki Davis Award from the Aspen Writers Foundation, and most recently the William Faulkner Award for the personal essay. Her poetry books include *Going Home, The Mask of Medusa, Making Bread at Midnight, How Heavy the Breath of God,* and *The Journals of Scheherazade.* She has also published a book of translations of the Cajun poet Jean Arceneaux, *Je Suis Cadien.* A book of lyric essays about growing up in Louisiana, *Swamp Songs: the Making of an Unruly Woman,* was published in 2003. Her most recent book is *Let it Be a Dark Roux: New and Selected Poems,* published by Autumn House Press in 2007.

DAVID STARKEY received his M.F.A. in Creative Writing from Louisiana State University in 1990, and is currently Poet Laureate of Santa Barbara and Director of the Creative Writing Program at Santa Barbara City College. Among his poetry collections are *Starkey's Book of States* (Boson Books, 2007), *Adventures of the Minor Poet* (Artamo Press, 2007), *Ways of Being Dead: New and Selected Poems* (Artamo Press, 2006), *David Starkey's Greatest Hits* (Pudding House, 2002) and *Fear of Everything,* winner of Palanquin Press's Spring 2000 chapbook contest. His most recent full-length collection of poetry is *A Few Things You Should Know about the Weasel* (Biblioasis, 2010). He has also written two textbooks: *Creative Writing: Four Genres in Brief* (Bedford/St. Martin's, 2008) and *Poetry Writing: Theme and Variations* (McGraw-Hill, 1999).

A native of Shreveport, Louisiana, JENNIFER STRANGE received the Master of Fine Arts at the University of Florida, studying primarily under poet and literary critic William Logan. She taught writing at Centenary College of Louisiana for ten years and serves as Assistant Editor to the Art House America blog. Her poems have appeared in *The Oxford American, Christianity and Literature,* and *Rock and Sling.*

GARLAND STROTHER is a native of Tensas Parish in north Louisiana. A retired librarian, he currently lives in River Ridge, Louisiana, near New Orleans. His poems have appeared most recently in *Tipton Poetry Journal, Innisfree Poetry Journal, New Verse News,* and *Cornbread Nation 5.*

L.E. SULLIVAN is a native of Baton Rouge, Louisiana, and resides in Nacogdoches, Texas. Currently a university student, she has not yet earned a journal publication, but works as an assistant for the literary journal *REAL* and as an editor for the undergraduate literary journal *Humid.*

JAN VILLARRUBIA's first poetry collection *Return to Bayou Lacombe* was recently published by Cinnamon Press in Wales. Her poems have been published in *Envoi, The Literary Review, Mississippi Valley Review, New Laurel Review* and many others. A New Orleans native, Villarrubia has won numerous fellowships, grants and awards for her plays, including a Theatre Fellowship from the Louisiana State Arts Council and the National Endowment for the Arts. Among her other full-length plays are *Miz Lena's Backyard* (Dramatic Publishing), *Odd Fellow's Rest* (Xavier Review Press) and *Yellow Roses That Big.*

TOM WHALEN's poems and prose poems have appeared in *Chelsea, Georgia Review, Hotel Amerika, Louisiana Literature, Mississippi Review, New Orleans Review, Seattle Review, Southern Review,* and elsewhere. His books of poetry include *Winter Coat* (Red Dust), *Strange Alleys* (Obscure Publications) and *Dolls* (winner of the 2006 Caketrain Chapbook Competition). His fiction, translations, and film and literary criticism have also appeared widely. For over two decades he directed the creative writing program at the New Orleans Center for Creative Arts and currently teaches film at the State Academy of Art and Design in Stuttgart, Germany. *The Birth of Death and Other Comedies: The Novels of Russell H. Greenan* appeared in 2011 with Dalkey Archive.

GAIL WHITE is the author of *Easy Marks* (David Robert Books), a finalist for the Poets Prize in 2008. She coedited the anthology *The Muse Strikes Back*, which has been reissued by Story Line Press. She is also the subject of Julie Kane's essay "Getting Serious About Gail White's Light Verse," which appeared in an early issue of *Mezzo Cammin*. Her website is www.gailwhite.org.

Margaret Media published ANGUS WOODWARD's collection of Louisiana short stories, *Down at the End of the River*, in 2008. His fiction and poetry have appeared in dozens of journals, including *Rhino, Louisiana Literature, Xavier Review, Alimentum, Night Sun,* and *Talking River Review*. Angus lives in Baton Rouge, where he teaches at Our Lady of the Lake College.

ANDY YOUNG is the co-editor of *Meena Magazine*, a bilingual Arabic-English literary journal, and teaches Creative Writing at New Orleans Center for Creative Arts. Her work has recently appeared in *Best New Poets 2009* (University of Virginia Press), *Callaloo, Guernica,* and *Language for a New Century: Contemporary Poetry from the Middle East, Asia & Beyond* (W.W. Norton & Co). She has published two chapbooks, *All Fires the Fire* (Faulkner House Books) and *mine* (Lavender Ink), and has been awarded the Faulkner Festival's Marble Faun Poetry Award, a Louisiana Division of the Arts Fellowship, a Surdna Artist-Teacher Fellowship, and writing residencies at the Santa Fe Arts Institute and the Vermont Studio Center. She was an invited guest to poetry festivals in Nicaragua and El Salvador. Her work has also appeared in electronic music, buses in Santa Fe, flamenco productions, jewelry designs by Jeanine Payer, and a tattoo parlor in Berlin.

ACKNOWLEDGEMENTS

The editors would like to thank all poets who contributed to this volume, as well as Michelle Nichols, who worked patiently and meticulously to proofread the work.

For contributors who supplied publication information, details are listed below. All poem copyrights have reverted back to respective authors, listed or otherwise, and Texas Review Press has permission to reprint poems included herein.

Ralph Adamo: "New Orleans Elegies," "Gift of the Guest" and "Us, Here, Ruled" first appeared in *Waterblind: Selected Poems* (Portals Press, 2002) **John Anderson**: "Three Things" first appeared in *Southern Review*. **Randy Bates**: "Dolphin Island" first appeared in *Prairie Schooner*; "Meteors" in *Southern Review*. **Glenn J. Bergeron II**: "Grand Isle 1996" first appeared in *Louisiana English Journal*; "Silent Retreat: Grand Cocteau, Louisiana" in *Louisiana Literature*. **John Biguenet**: "Scrimshaw" first appeared in *North American Review*; "Nine Nudes" in Boulevard; "The Wall Behind the Mirror" in *New Orleans Review*. **John Blair**: "Oleander" previously appeared in *The Green Girls* (Pleiades P, 2003); "Winter Storm, New Orleans" in *Poetry* and in *The Green Girls*; "The Dogs of Grass" in *Arts and Letters*. **Darrell Bourque**: "Light Theology and the Persimmon Tree" appeared in *Ordinary Light: New and Selected Poems* (U of Louisiana at Lafayette P, 2010); "The Black Door at Arnaudville" and "Scratch" in *Call and Response* (Texas Review P, 2009). **Allen Braden**: "Walker Evans" first appeared in *Interdisciplinary Humanities*; "Flight Theory" in *A Wreath of Down and Drops of Blood* (U of Georgia P, 2010). **Catharine Savage Brosman**: "Tree in Winter" appeared in *Trees in a Park* (Chicory Bloom P, 2010); "Fire in the Mind" and "On the Bayou" in *Breakwater* (Mercer U P, 2009). **Steven C. Brown, Jr.**: "Wormlight," "June's Entomology," and "Animalia" appeared in *Moth and Bonelight* (21st Editions, 2010). **Liz Burk**: "Learning to Love Louisiana" first appeared in *The Wisconsin Review*. **Kelly Cherry**: "The Bride of Quietness" appeared in *Loves and Agnostics* (Carnegie Mellon P, 1995); "Sharks" in *Relativity: A Point of View* (LSU P, 1977; Carnegie Mellon P, 1999); and "Two Roses" in *Natural Theology* (LSU P, 1988). **William Bedford Clark**: "'Katrina refugees return – weigh future'" appeared in *Blue Norther and Other Poems* (Texas Review P, 2010). **Carlos Colón**: "His Last Letter" first appeared in *Louisiana Literature*; "Refracted Memory" in North of New Orleans. **Peter Cooley**: "To Christ Our Lord" first appeared in *The Kenyon Review*; "Downtown" in *The Oxford American*. **Kevin Cutrer**: "Lord's Own Anointed" first appeared in *The Hudson Review* and later in *A Face to Meet the Faces: An Anthology of Contemporary Persona Poetry*; "On Dale's Role in the Christmas Pageant" in *The Dark Horse*; "Butcher" in *Texas Review*. **John Doucet**: "Le Charivari de Celestin Joseph Doucet" first appeared in *Uncommonplace: An Anthology of Contemporary Louisiana Poets* (LSU P, 1998). **John Freeman**: "August Green: A Baptism" first appeared as part of the Pygmy Forest Broadside Series in 2000 and later in *Visions International*; "The Yearning: Late October" in *The Neovictorian/Cochlea*; "After Katrina" in *Desire Street*. **Jesse Graves**: "The Night Café: North Rendon, New Orleans," "Faubourg Marigny," and "Bayou Storm in Summer" appeared in *Tennessee Landscape with Blighted Pine* (Texas Review P, 2011). **Ashley Mace Havird**: "Dirt Eaters" first appeared in *Shenandoah*; "Sideshow" in *Southern Review*; "Resurrection: Ivorybill" in *Southern Humanities Review*. **David Havird**: "A

Wind of Goats" and "Smoking in Bed" appeared in *Penelope's Design: Fourteen Poems* (Texas Review P, 2010); "Smoking in Bed" first appeared in the *Yale Review*. **Ava Leavell Haymon:** "How One Became Two" first appeared in *Louisiana Literature* and in *Why the House Is Made of Gingerbread* (LSU P, 2010); "All the Men in My Family Hunt" in *Louisiana Literature* and in *Kitchen Heat* (LSU P, 2006). **Carolyn Hembree:** "Rigging a Chevy into a Time Machine. . ." first appeared in *Colorado Review*. **Julie Kane:** "Ode to the Big Muddy" and "Egrets" appeared in *From Rhythm & Booze*. Copyright 2003 by Julie Kane. Used with permission of the University of Illinois Press. **Richard Katrovas:** "Blue's Body" and "Love Poem for an Enemy" appeared in volumes of poetry published by Wesleyan U P or Carnegie Mellon P. **David Kirby:** "Psychodynamic Electrohelmet" first appeared in *Granta*; "On Learning I Share a Birthday. . ." in *Boulevard*; "Why I Don't Drink Before Readings" in *Southern Review*. **Bill Lavender:** "For Niyi Osundare" first appeared in *The Pinch*. **Martha McFerren:** "Archaeology at Midnight" first appeared in *Poetry*. **Michael McManus:** "Out There" first appeared in *Atlanta Review*; "Riding a Horse" in *Texas Review*. **Kevin Meaux:** "My Grandfather's Trees" appeared in *Myths of Electricity* (Texas Review P, 2005). **Kay Murphy:** "for my Books" first appeared in *Copper Nickel*. **David Middleton:** "The Vision" appeared in *The Burning Fields* (LSU P, 1991). **Stella Nesanovich:** "Eggplant" was published as a broadside by Yellow Flag Press, 2010; "Oyster Shuckers" first appeared in *Louisiana Literature*; "Revisiting New Orleans in a Season of Joy" in the 2008 *Jubilee Anthology*, published by by Nicholls State U. **James Nolan:** "Over the Oysters" first appeared in *Maple Leaf Rag III: An Anthology of Poems* (Portals P, 2006); "King Midas Blues" in *Meena: A Bilingual Journal of Arts and Letters*; "Acts of God" in *Callaloo: A Journal of African Diaspora Arts and Letters*. **Biljana D. Obradovic:** "Life's Little Disruptions" appeared in *Little Disruptions* (Niš Cultural Center, 2010). **Sue Owen:** "Dead Man Floats" appeared in *The Devil's Cookbook* (LSU P, 2007); "Dead Man Floats," "Hurricane and Its Eye," and "Tell About the Trees" appeared in *Louisiana Literature*. **Melinda Palacio:** "The Fisherman and the Evening News" first appeared in *San Pedro River Review*. **Wyatt Prunty:** "Water," "The Name," and "The Vegetable Garden" appeared in *Unarmed and Dangerous* (The Johns Hopkins U P, 2000); **Brad Richard:** "Dirt-Dauber's Nest" appeared in *Habitations* (Portals Press, 2000); "The Cooling Board, 1929" and "I Take a Book from the Shelf" in *Motion Studies* (The Word Works Books, 2011) **David Rowe:** "Salamander; or, Splitting the World Asunder" first appeared in *Salamander; or, Splitting the World Asunder* (Verna Press, 2009). **William Ryan:** "Where to Begin" and "Trouble in Heaven" appeared in *To Die in Latin* (Lynx House P, 1994). **Martha Serpas:** "The Water," "Psalm at High Tide," and "The Dirty Side of the Storm" all appeared in *The Dirty Side of the Storm*, Copyright 2007 and used with permission of W.W. Norton. **Katherine Soniat:** "Bright Blessed Days" first appeareed in *Chiron Review*. **Brian Spears:** "Up South" and "I-55" appeared in *Louisiana Literature* and *A Witness in Exile* (Louisiana Literature P, 2010). **Sheryl St. Germain:** "Addiction" and "Cajun" appeared in *Let It Be a Dark Roux: New and Selected Poems* (Autumn House P, 2007). **Garland Strother:** "Pulling Cotton" first appeared in *Arkansas Review*; "The Hunter" in *Common Ground Review*; "The Pool Hall" in *Tipton Poetry Journal*. **Jan Villarrubia:** "Cows on High" appeared in *Return to Bayou Lacombe* (Cinnamon P, 2008). **Tom Whalen:** "Tomato" first appeared in *Kestrel*; "Getting Back to Him" in *Southern Review*; "Tomato" and "Getting Back to Him" later appeared in *Winter Coat* (Red Dust, 1998). **Angus Woodward:** "Azalea Street Winter" first appeared in *Bellingham Review*.